PRAYERS TO
THE SAINTS
(UPDATED EDITION)

James H. Kurt

© 2007, 2019 James H. Kurt
All Rights Reserved.

Children of Light Publications.
jameshkurt@gmail.com

Original version published by AuthorHouse.

No part of this book may be reproduced, stored in a retrieval system, or transmitted by any means without the written permission of the author.

ISBN: 978-1-7332154-2-8

Nihil Obstat:
Rev. Frederick L. Miller S.T.D.
Censor Librorum
July 11, 2019

Imprimatur:
+ Cardinal Joseph W. Tobin C.Ss.R.
Archbishop of Newark, New Jersey
July 30, 2019

The **Nihil Obstat** and **Imprimatur** are official declarations that a book or pamphlet is free of doctrinal error. No implication is contained therein that those who have granted the **Nihil Obstat** and **Imprimatur** agree with the contents, opinions, or statements expressed.

Cover art by James Kurt.

Saints chosen in accord with the Latin Rite Catholic calendar
for the United States as of 2019.
(plus two)

"Come then, Lord, and help your people,
bought with the price of your own blood,
and bring us with your saints
to glory everlasting."

from the
Te Deum

Index of Saints

Achilleus (May 12) 67
Adalbert (April 23) 56
Agatha (February 5) 24
Agnes (January 21) 12
Albert the Great (November 15) 207
All Saints (November 1) 200
Aloysius Gonzaga (June 21) 97
Alphonsus Liguori (August 1) 130
Ambrose (December 7) 223
André Bessette (January 6) 6
Andrew (November 30) 218
Andrew Dung-Lac (November 24) 216
Andrew Kim Taegon (September 20) 168
Angela Merici (January 27) 18
Anne (July 26) 124
Annunciation (March 25) 45
Anselm (April 21) 54
Ansgar (February 3) 23
Anthony Mary Claret (October 24) 197
Anthony Mary Zaccaria (July 5) 109
Anthony of Padua (June 13) 95
Anthony the Abbot (January 17) 9
Apollinaris (July 20) 118
Assumption (August 15) 143
Athanasius (May 2) 65
Augustine (August 28) 154
Augustine of Canterbury (May 27) 81
Augustine Zhao Rong (July 9) 111
Barnabas (June 11) 94
Bartholomew (August 24) 150
Basil the Great (January 2) 3
Bede the Venerable (May 25) 77

iv

Benedict (July 11) 112
Bernard (August 20) 146
Bernardine of Siena (May 20) 74
Blaise (February 3) 22
Bonaventure (July 15) 114
Boniface (June 5) 91
Bridget (July 23) 121
Bruno (October 6) 182
Cajetan (August 7) 135
Callistus I (October 14) 186
Camillus de Lellis (July 18) 117
Casimir (March 4) 37
Catherine of Alexandria (November 25) 217
Catherine of Siena (April 29) 61
Cecilia (November 22) 213
Chair of St. Peter (February 22) 33
Charles Borromeo (November 4) 202
Charles Lwanga (June 3) 90
Christopher Magallanes (May 21) 75
Clare (August 11) 139
Clement I (November 23) 214
Columban (November 23) 215
Conversion of St. Paul (January 25) 16
Cornelius (September 16) 165
Cosmas (September 26) 171
Cyprian (September 16) 165
Cyril (February 14) 30
Cyril of Alexandria (June 27) 101
Cyril of Jerusalem (March 18) 42
Damasus I (December 11) 226
Damian (September 26) 171
Damien de Veuster (May 10) 67
Denis (October 9) 184
Dominic (August 8) 136
Elizabeth Ann Seton (January 4) 4

v

Elizabeth of Hungary (November 17) 210
Elizabeth of Portugal (July 5 in USA) 108
Ephrem (June 9) 93
Eusebius of Vercelli (August 2) 131
Fabian (January 20) 10
Felicity (March 7) 38
Fidelis of Sigmaringen (April 24) 57
First Martyrs of the Holy Roman Church (June 30) 104
Frances of Rome (March 9) 40
Frances Xavier Cabrini (November 13) 206
Francis de Sales (January 24) 14
Francis of Assisi (October 4) 180
Francis of Paola (April 2) 48
Francis Xavier (December 3) 220
Gabriel (September 29) 175
George (April 23) 55
Gertrude (November 16) 209
Gregory VII (May 25) 78
Gregory Nazianzen (January 2) 3
Gregory the Great (September 3) 158
Guardian Angels (October 2) 179
Hedwig (October 16) 189
Henry (July 13) 113
Hilary (January 13) 8
Hippolytus (August 13) 140
Holy Family (Sunday in the Octave of Christmas or Dec. 30) 236
Holy Innocents (December 28) 234
Ignatius of Antioch (October 17) 191
Ignatius of Loyola (July 31) 127
Immaculate Conception (December 8) 224
Immaculate Heart of Mary (Sat. foll. 2nd Sun. after Pentecost).. 84
Irenaeus (June 28) 102
Isaac Jogues (October 19) 193
Isidore (April 4) 49
Isidore the Farmer (May 15) 72

James, the Greater (July 25)	123
James, the Less (May 3)	66
Jane Frances de Chantal (August 12)	140
Januarius (September 19)	167
Jerome (September 30)	176
Jerome Emiliani (February 8)	26
Joachim (July 26)	124
John (December 27)	233
John I (May 18)	73
John XXIII (October 11)	186
John Baptist de la Salle (April 7)	51
John Bosco (January 31)	20
John Chrysostom (September 13)	163
John de Brébeuf (October 19)	193
John Eudes (August 19)	145
John Fisher (June 22)	99
John Leonardi (October 9)	184
John Mary Vianney (August 4)	133
John Neumann (January 5)	5
John of Capistrano (October 23)	195
John of Damascus (December 4)	221
John of God (March 8)	39
John of Kanty (December 23)	231
John of the Cross (December 14)	229
John Paul II (October 22)	195
Josaphat (November 12)	205
Joseph Calasanz (August 25)	152
Joseph, Husband of Mary (March 19)	43
Josephine Bakhita (February 8)	27
Joseph the Worker (May 1)	64
Juan Diego (December 9)	225
Jude (October 28)	198
Junípero Serra (July 1)	106
Justin (June 1)	88
Kateri Tekakwitha (July 14)	114

Katharine Drexel (March 3) 36
Lawrence (August 10) 138
Lawrence of Brindisi (July 21) 119
Lawrence Ruiz (September 28) 174
Leo the Great (November 10) 203
Louis Mary de Montfort (April 28) 60
Louis of France (August 25) 151
Lucy (December 13) 228
Luke (October 18) 192
Marcellinus (June 2) 89
Margaret Mary Alacoque (October 16) 190
Margaret of Scotland (November 16) 208
Maria Goretti (July 6) 110
Maria Faustina (October 5) 181
Marianne Cope (January 23) 14
Mark (April 25) 58
Martha (July 29) 125
Martin I (April 13) 53
Martin de Porres (November 3) 201
Martin of Tours (November 11) 204
Martyrdom of St. John the Baptist (August 29) 155
Mary, Mother of God (January 1) 2
Mary, Mother of the Church (Monday after Pentecost) 84
Mary Magdalene (July 22) 120
Mary Magdalene de´ Pazzi (May 25) 79
Matthew (September 21) 169
Matthias (May 14) 71
Maximilian Mary Kolbe (August 14) 141
Methodius (February 14) 30
Michael (September 29) 175
Monica (August 27) 153
Most Holy Name of Mary (September 12) 162
Nativity of John the Baptist (June 24) 100
Nativity of Mary (September 8) 159
Nereus (May 12) 67

Nicholas (December 6) 222
Norbert (June 6) 92
Our Lady of Fatima (May 13) 70
Our Lady of Guadalupe (December 12) 227
Our Lady of Lourdes (February 11) 29
Our Lady of Mount Carmel (July 16) 116
Our Lady of Sorrows (September 15) 164
Our Lady of the Rosary (October 7) 183
Pancras (May 12) 69
Patrick (March 17) 41
Paul (June 29) 103
Paul VI (May 29) 82
Paul Chong Hasang (September 20) 168
Paul Miki (February 6) 25
Paul of the Cross (October 20) 194
Paulinus of Nola (June 22) 98
Perpetua (March 7) 38
Peter (June 29) 103
Peter Canisius (December 21) 230
Peter Chanel (April 28) 59
Peter Chrysologus (July 30) 126
Peter Claver (September 9) 161
Peter Damian (February 21) 32
Peter Julian Eymard (August 2) 132
Peter, Martyr (June 2) 89
Philip (May 3) 66
Philip Neri (May 26) 80
Pio of Pietrelcina (September 23) 170
Pius V (April 30) 62
Pius X (August 21) 147
Polycarp (February 23) 34
Pontian (August 13) 140
Presentation of Mary (November 21) 212
Queenship of Mary (August 22) 148
Raphael (September 29) 175

Raymond of Peñafort (January 7) 7
Rita of Cascia (May 22) 76
Robert Bellarmine (September 17) 166
Romuald (June 19) 96
Rose of Lima (August 23) 149
Rose Philippine Duchesne (November 18) 211
Scholastica (February 10) 28
Sebastian (January 20) 11
Seven Founders of the Order of Servites (February 17) 31
Sharbel Makhluf (July 24) 122
Simon (October 28) 198
Sixtus II (August 7) 134
Stanislaus (April 11) 52
Stephen (December 26) 232
Stephen of Hungary (August 16) 144
Sylvester I (December 31) 237
Teresa Benedicta of the Cross (August 9) 137
Teresa of Calcutta (September 5) 159
Teresa of Jesus (October 15) 187
Thérèse of the Child Jesus (October 1) 178
Thomas (July 3) 106
Thomas Aquinas (January 28) 19
Thomas Becket (December 29) 235
Thomas More (June 22) 99
Timothy (January 26) 17
Titus (January 26) 17
Turibius de Mogrovejo (March 23) 44
Vincent (January 23) 13
Vincent de Paul (September 27) 172
Vincent Ferrer (April 5) 50
Visitation (May 31) 82
Wenceslaus (September 28) 173

JANUARY

Prayers to the Saints

Mary, Mother of God (January 1)

O Blessed Virgin

in whose womb was conceived

the only Son of God,

who by such grace

has brought salvation

to our race…

What faith is yours

in God the Father!

What power is upon you

by the Holy Spirit!

What unutterable wonder we find

in your Son!

How is it one of our own number

could give birth

to our Creator?

Such glorious union

with the Godhead

we could never merit

nor discover

except that the Lord

has chosen you —

pray this day

He shall be born in us, too.

January

Sts. Basil the Great and Gregory Nazianzen
(January 2)

O bishops and doctors,

O brothers so united in Christ,

united in your desire

to find His wisdom

and live His virtue,

for you what mattered

but to be like Christ?

All you would have given up

to find His way;

nothing of this world

did you wish

but to leave it

behind.

One in heart and mind,

one in word and work

and in the food of which you partook…

how blessed it is

when men live as brothers,

when nothing they desire

but the other's good –

teach us this way of union

in the love of God.

Prayers to the Saints

St. Elizabeth Ann Seton (January 4)

O mother through marriage

and religious Mother,

who indeed became mother of many,

many sisters whom you led

in the faith

and many children whom you taught

in your schools —

in your wisdom

teach many still

the path of Christ,

the way of charity He has trod,

that renewed will those be

who call you Mother,

and instructed well

those in their classrooms

throughout the land.

What should we teach our children,

dear Mother?

Have we not forgotten the lesson of Christ?

Pray for us, I beg,

this day,

that the way and the truth

we shall follow.

St. John Neumann (January 5)

O shepherd who walked

in the humble stead

of your flock,

who worked so diligently

among those in your care,

speaking to their hearts;

you who gathered into schools

the little ones,

who saw to the education

of the children…

and all this in a foreign land —

pray for the country in which you ministered,

that its lambs

once again be raised

in the faith

and its strangers

be once again shepherded

by one as anxious as you

for their well-being.

Here let us find the grace of Christ

to redeem

the lowly

and the lost.

Prayers to the Saints

St. André Bessette (January 6)

O friend of the lowly,

humble child of St. Joseph,

servant of the poor

and counsel to the afflicted

through whom the Lord worked miracles…

how He blessed your ignorance

with His wisdom,

your weakness with His strength;

unattached

to this passing world,

you drew souls

to the world to come –

pray we be as poor and lowly

as the dust you swept each day,

as the Child Jesus

in the manger at Bethlehem.

Pray we, too, have ears

to hear and answer

the needs of others

and that good St. Joseph

will hold us in his arms

and carry us with you

unto Heaven.

St. Raymond of Peñafort (January 7)

O redeemer of captive slaves,

those enslaved to sin

and those enslaved

by the clutches of the world —

preach to us this day

the freedom found

under the Cross of Christ

and in the repentance of heart

blessed by the grace

upon the Church.

Teach us well

the path to Heaven,

which is wrought not in comfort and peace

but in struggle against sin,

in the laying down of our lives

before our persecutors.

Ransom us from wayward

thoughts and actions,

and from the snares

of the adversary

who waits for our misstep.

In Christ alone

may we find our rest.

Prayers to the Saints

St. Hilary (January 13)

O shepherd and doctor

of God's holy Church,

is this not what you would declare

with all your breath

to the ends of the earth:

"Jesus is the Son of God

and God Himself"?

Would you not proclaim

the true light of Scripture

and the Word, the Light,

become flesh in our midst?

Know, O saint of the Lord,

that your words reach our ears

and our hearts

even to this day,

and this day we proclaim you holy

and your words true —

continue to speak to us;

please intercede for us,

that the Truth you declared

so fearlessly

will be taken up again

by those in His stead today.

St. Anthony the Abbot (January 17)

O father of monks

and all who would give themselves

completely to the Lord,

you who have been so obedient

to the word of God,

to His call

to sell everything,

to renounce all possessions

and follow Him —

how we need your prayers

this day,

when love for material things

possesses our very bodies

and souls,

when prayer and penance

seem things of the distant past.

Make present to us

the blessed call of the Lord,

the renunciation of the world,

that we too might find

the riches of Heaven

you knew so well.

Pray we give up all for God.

Prayers to the Saints

St. Fabian (January 20)

O Holy Father of the Church,

Pastor of the sheep of our Lord

who have given your life freely

for the Name of Christ

and its spreading

throughout the earth,

you whose blood was shed

by the persecutors

of the body

but whose soul

was ever in the Hand of God –

pray our lives

shall be lived in integrity

and our death correspond,

that a blessed witness

we too shall give

to the glory of God

and His Son Jesus Christ,

and so lead others

to that same glory.

May none of the flock

or their shepherds

fear the sacrifice of their lives.

St. Sebastian (January 20)

O soldier for Christ

who sought with such courage

to embrace His Cross,

to die a death

worthy of such a Lord,

you whose heart

was so set

on imitating the suffering

only He knew

and so were rewarded

with the crown of martyrdom –

where is our courage;

where is our strength?

Pray for us,

O warrior of our Lord and God,

that our lives

may bear witness

to approach your own,

that we shall not shrink

from the Cross before us

but with your same zeal

seek to make it our own.

Pray the blood of Christ upon us.

Prayers to the Saints

St. Agnes (January 21)

O holy virgin martyr,

O innocent child

who offered your life

more freely than a bride

to her husband,

more courageously than a warrior

in battle,

who though lacking in years

was not lacking in faith

nor desire to honor

your only Spouse…

you who were honored

by the Fathers of the Church

and are remembered to this day

as a holy offering,

a lamb of God sacrificed in flames

yet professing ever

your love for Christ —

but a small measure of your courage

would save our souls.

Pray but a drop of His blood

we may know

falling from our veins.

St. Vincent (January 23)

O martyr of the Lord extraordinaire

who suffered unspeakable torture

but was not bowed

by such savagery,

who spoke of great faith,

singing of God's glory

even as your limbs

were crushed,

even as all the brutality

the world could inflict

sought to break

your spirit —

help us to conquer the world

as you have done,

as the Lord has done in you,

not to be afraid

but rather to serve

our Savior and His Cross

in joy

as His blessed disciples;

pray we, too, shall enter the heavenly gates

open to those in whom the Spirit speaks

even unto death.

Prayers to the Saints

St. Marianne Cope (January 23)

O lover of the least,

the most wretched of society,

whom you embraced

when no one else would;

how like St. Francis you were

in your care for the lepers,

in your living the Gospel

as an image of Christ:

He was hungry and you fed Him,

thirsty and you gave Him drink,

naked and you clothed Him

and cared for Him when He was sick —

pray our hearts will burn

with the same sacrificial love

you bore so well

for those most abandoned,

that truly we shall see Christ in them

and welcome Him

into our homes…

may their suffering be our own.

How else shall we become holy?

How else shall we be welcomed

into the kingdom with you?

St. Francis de Sales (January 24)

O most devout spiritual guide,

great pastor of your flock

and of all souls,

you who speak to us

even this day

with your words of wisdom

and blessed direction –

pray every branch

of Jesus' vine

may aspire to His perfection;

in whatever state we find ourselves,

let us set our hearts

on loving the Lord

and serving Him and neighbor

prayerfully.

Teach us to pray faithfully,

to offer our lives

in all situations,

all for the glory of God.

Our call may we hear

and heed by your intercession,

following the Christ and carrying His Cross

as He leads.

Prayers to the Saints

Conversion of St. Paul (January 25)

O you who persecuted

the Church of God

but then preached the faith

in earnest,

you upon whom

abundant mercy fell,

whose weakness became strength

as each day in bearing

extraordinary torments

you grew closer to the Lord —

show us the way

to Heaven.

Pray we fall continually

from our horse,

from our pride,

and allow Jesus

to change our lives.

Pray repentance

be our constant food,

that the love of Jesus

and His forgiveness

we shall ever know

in greater measure.

Sts. Timothy and Titus
(January 26)

O blessed disciples of Paul

and shepherds of the Church

who imitated so well

your father in the faith

who imitated only

the Lord Jesus Christ

and thirsted for His Cross —

pray this holy Apostle

be our father, too,

and you with him,

that we too might embrace the Cross;

teach us the sound doctrine

handed on to you

that we may hand it on

and all souls

might fight the good fight

and run the race with Jesus

unto eternal life.

Pray for all the shepherds of the Church

that they be faithful

as you have been

to rightful authority.

Prayers to the Saints

St. Angela Merici (January 27)

O holy virgin

and spiritual mother

to the poorest of girls,

whom you protected and guided

in wisdom and love,

keeping them from the snares

of the world

and raising them in Christ;

you who fulfilled so well

the twofold call

to love God and save souls —

pray for those

who so easily go astray

this day

in a world of great corruption,

where souls are in danger

of being captured

by the wiles of Satan and sin;

and pray, too,

that there shall be many

who desire as you have,

with the living love of God,

to bring them into His fold.

St. Thomas Aquinas (January 28)

O wise doctor of the Church

who ate the bread of angels

in your long hours

of prayer and study and writing

and shared with us

the knowledge you gained

of the sublime truth of God,

shedding the light of reason

upon the faith we hold so dear —

teach us this day

to know God

that we might better love and serve Him,

that we might not be blind

to His presence in our midst,

to the holiness to which He calls us.

Pray we shall enter into

His Cross, His love, His obedience;

pray we, too, might have knowledge,

true knowledge of His grace

and the everlasting life

which is ours in Him…

and pray the Lord send us holy teachers

to fill your shoes.

Prayers to the Saints

St. John Bosco (January 31)

O teacher and father

of the children in your care,

in whose hands

they were not abandoned

but held in patience

by Christ's love —

teach us, too,

to have that same patience,

to have that same love

for those the Lord places

in our care,

that anger shall be banished

from our hearts and our minds,

that the wisdom of Christ's sacrifice

you taught and lived

we too might embody,

and so serve

in raising the kingdom of Heaven

among the children of this earth.

And pray that we, too,

may know the Lord's gentle word and touch

upon our own souls

and so grow into His likeness.

FEBRUARY

Prayers to the Saints

St. Blaise (February 3)

O shepherd whom we invoke

for the healing of throats,

you who suffered torments

for the sake of the Name

and embraced death

as leader of His flock —

open our throats

to speak of Jesus,

to declare His goodness and glory,

the salvation that comes

only through Him.

Let us not fear

our persecutors

nor shrink from the threats

of the mighty

but stand fast

in the Lord's healing grace,

confident that His every blessing

will keep us well

and on the path

that leads only to Heaven.

Pray all sickness flee from us

this day and forever.

February

St. Ansgar (February 3)

O bringer of light

to many nations,

you who struggled on

for the souls placed in your care

that all might know the Christ

for whom you toiled,

endlessly seeking

to convert obstinate hearts —

may your zeal

inspire missionaries this day

to go forth selflessly

proclaiming the Gospel to all,

bearing witness to the Lord

in the cross they bear

in season and out of season;

whether producing much fruit

or being rejected,

may their hearts be set on the Word

and the love of God

for His children.

Pray especially those lands you led to Christ

will turn again

to the one true light.

Prayers to the Saints

St. Agatha (February 5)

O good child of God

who gave your life so willingly

for the sake of Christ

and so wore His holy blood

upon your robes,

you who were blessed

to remain ever faithful to the Lord

even as those around you

turned from His presence —

pray for us this day

that our lives too

may be holy and blessed

as your own,

that we too might give witness to the Lord

with the same pure love

you did so readily show.

Pray we shall be wed to the Spouse

you so intimately knew

and thus become one with Him

and all His saints in Heaven.

May our lives also be good,

may they also be godly,

and may we, too, stand as others fall.

February

St. Paul Miki and Companions
(February 6)

O proclaimers of the faith

even unto death,

death on a cross,

you who have followed

in the way of our Lord

so completely,

loving your enemies

even as they killed you,

encouraging your brothers

even with your last breath —

may the blood you shed

not be forgotten

by those of the nation in which you preached

and by all souls who seek God;

may it nourish the land

and bring it to bear much fruit

unto Heaven.

Pray that we who are so fearful here

may find the faith and courage

you displayed

and so be blessed with the same grace

that imparts the peace of the kingdom.

Prayers to the Saints

St. Jerome Emiliani (February 8)

O soldier for the Lord

and servant of the poor

who trusted in God alone

and gave your life

for those in need –

may we, too, become friends of the one Lord,

purified of all dross

by the trials we endure

and by doing His will

in this world.

His children let us become

as we care for the children

most in need,

those who seem abandoned

by Him.

His hands and His heart

let us be,

that in such love

we shall be free

of all fear and separation

from the Father

and so dwell with those we serve

in the peace of Heaven.

St. Josephine Bakhita (February 8)

O innocent soul,

pure as an angel,

meek as a lamb,

from slavery you were taken

to the house of God,

where freedom you found

in faith in the Lord —

pray for the freedom of all slaves

chained in soul or body,

that they shall be released

from the snares of this world

to walk at liberty with Jesus.

Pray His goodness reign

in all His children,

in all who would be

gentle as this Lamb;

may all those in need of His grace

hear His Word proclaimed,

and in His blood

be redeemed.

And pray His Mother watch over

all who are near or far from Him,

till they enter His presence.

Prayers to the Saints

St. Scholastica (February 10)

O holy virgin,

sister to St. Benedict

and to us all

by virtue of your blessed vow

to our holy Lord —

pray all souls shall consecrate themselves

to Jesus and to His love,

that upon the heart of every man

shall be the desire to serve Him well

and so find His blessing.

May we all delight in the spiritual life,

straining ever toward Heaven,

the things of this earth

but means to union

with our Lord and Savior.

Though we may not all be monks and nuns,

let us yet know His holiness,

let us yet discover

the God who is love,

that all our lives

shall be lived in Him

until we become

one with His saints in light.

Our Lady of Lourdes (February 11)

O lovely Lady who appeared to Bernadette,

Mary, Blessed Virgin and Mother of our Lord —

let our eyes, too, see your beauty

and hear your voice

calling us to pray for sinners,

calling us to come to you with our prayers

and to wash ourselves clean

in the water you provide

through Jesus your Son.

O Immaculate Conception,

so pure, so full of grace,

cleanse all our sickness from us;

let us be immersed

in the bath of purity

that washes us of sin,

that makes us whole

in the sight of God.

If we but had innocent hearts

we would see you,

we would remember the blessing you are

to all faithful souls…

O let us come to you

and find the grace we need this day.

Prayers to the Saints

Sts. Cyril and Methodius
(February 14)

O brothers in the faith

who brought that same faith

to the peoples

entrusted to your care,

who extended the reach of the Church,

gathering in lands

under her holy roof

and into her blessed arms…

faithful you were unto death

in proclaiming the word of God —

please pray that we, too,

shall be holy brothers of Christ,

offering our work, our lives,

for the sake of the nations

yet to be called

into His fold,

for the sake of peoples

unfamiliar with His Word,

that the heavenly kingdom

may come to fulfillment

and all be made one

in God's presence.

February

Seven Founders of the Order of Servites
(February 17)

O seven men

who lived as one

in service of the Lord

under the mantle of Our Lady,

you who left everything of this world,

all you bought and sold,

that you might discover the riches

of Heaven:

to the mountain you went

to find perfection –

to the mountain let us come

to live with God.

Led by the prompting of our Lord and Lady,

let us, too, be fruitful on this plane,

founded in humility and love and poverty,

living as one in the Body of Christ,

freely giving our lives

and so knowing the blessing

of the virtues upon which you fed.

Pray for us through our Mother

that we too follow

the call of her Son.

Prayers to the Saints

St. Peter Damian (February 21)

O blessed reformer of the Church

who by a holy austerity

cleansed your soul

of the corruption of this world

and served by example

to lead others to a religious life —

teach us this day

of the chastising hand of God

and the suffering which leads

to joy,

that in the will of the Lord

we might all be purged

of our dross

and come to the kingdom of Heaven.

Pray that we, too, might realize

and so benefit from

the blessing upon us

when our souls are lashed

with pains

that threaten sorrow,

for the Lord does but wish to lift us

from the sinfulness of this passing earth

to the consolation of His presence.

Chair of St. Peter (February 22)

O Rock of the Church,

leader of God's people

to whom the Father has revealed

the divinity of His Son

and on whom the Son has therefore

built His Church,

giving you the keys to the kingdom,

the power to bind and loose

both on earth and in Heaven,

that the ship you steer

might conquer all Satan's power

by the power of the Spirit

with which you serve your brothers,

secure in the blessed protection

and guidance of the Lord —

pray the Church you do yet lead

shall fulfill the call

the Christ has placed

upon every soul

and that we shall come to our heavenly home

in the light of the Messiah.

Pray we shall indeed be strong

and give faithful witness to our Savior.

Prayers to the Saints

St. Polycarp (February 23)

O disciple of John

and shepherd who drank deeply

of the cup of Christ's suffering,

you who bore both

the burden of a long life

and the pain of a violent death

yet remained faithful

till the end —

pray that the fire into which we are cast

we may also endure

as the sacrifice of Jesus

and so find it fruitful,

and so find it blessed...

and so rejoice in the witness

we are granted to give

in the Name of our Savior.

May the offering of our lives

join with your own and all the saints'

in rising as holy incense

to the throne of God

and serve as witness,

to the eyes that behold us,

of the Lord's great power and love.

MARCH

Prayers to the Saints

St. Katharine Drexel (March 3)

O mother to the poor

and disadvantaged,

missionary to those in your own country

isolated from their neighbors

because of the color of their skin,

some who lived upon the land

long before those who oppressed them,

others brought to this land

in chains…

you who sought to break the chains

of ignorance and poverty,

who gave your treasure

and the riches of your soul

that those without

might find a home –

pray for souls still disadvantaged

by poverty or ignorance;

pray that those with

and those without

might meet as one,

as brothers before the Lord

here on earth

and in the heavenly kingdom.

St. Casimir (March 4)

O patron of the impoverished

who though son of a king

counted yourself among

the poor in spirit,

you whose love abundantly flowed

to all in need,

who sought the purity

of our Blessed Mother,

who thirsted for our Lord

in the Blessed Sacrament,

who devoted yourself

to prayer

and constant works of charity –

teach us this day to be pure

and set our hearts

on serving the poor

that we too might come

to share the kingdom

with all God's children,

all those who empty themselves

of the things of this world

to find the grace

of Heaven.

Prayers to the Saints

Sts. Perpetua and Felicity
(March 7)

O blessed martyrs

who willingly and happily

suffered a cruel death

by the teeth of beasts

and the point of a sword,

all for love of Jesus —

how can we match your faith;

where shall we find the strength

you displayed

in ecstasy at tortures

devised by the wicked of this earth,

and can we call ourselves Christian

otherwise?

Pray for us, dear martyrs,

that the Lord will bless us

with such favor

as you have known

and we, too, will be enabled

to stand in joy

even in the face of the severest persecution,

even at the time of our death…

even then may Heaven be with us.

St. John of God (March 8)

O servant of love

whom the angels knew

to be of God

for your blessed care

of the poor and the sick

and all the needy pilgrims

who came to you in abundance

that you might be the greater blest

by what you did for the least

of Christ's brothers,

you who turned from the world

to absolute service of the Lord

and complete trust in His providence —

please pray that our hearts

may be enlarged

and we find the grace

to lay down our lives so freely

for the needs of others,

for their well-being,

that as we welcome all who come to us

we might ourselves be welcomed

in our misery

into the loving arms of Jesus.

Prayers to the Saints

St. Frances of Rome (March 9)

O patient and loving soul

who cared for both

the physical and spiritual needs

of the poor and the sick,

who with a gentle word

would rebuke sins

and heal division,

and with a gentle touch

bind the wounds

and smooth the beds

of the ill

in your home and in hospital,

who saw that remedies for the soul,

the Bread of life and holy Confession,

were available, too,

through the hands of a priest —

who cares as deeply and fully

for the needs of God's children

this day?

Increase their number;

pray the Lord touch all souls

with your same patient affection,

with the love only He knows.

March

St. Patrick (March 17)

O great apostle to the nations

who gave up your birthright of freedom

for the benefit of others,

who went forth in faith,

Christ ever above you and before you

and all around to protect you,

who were brought through trial

to do His will

in bringing God to unbelievers,

you who never doubted –

pray that we, too, shall spend ourselves

for the sake of the Gospel

and all souls

yet to be gathered to the Lord,

that indeed from east and west

men shall come

and sit with Abraham, Isaac, and Jacob

in the kingdom of our God,

that from the ends of the earth

one people shall be drawn to Him…

and let us do all

without concern for persecution,

with the heart of a shepherd you had.

Prayers to the Saints

St. Cyril of Jerusalem (March 18)

O steadfast teacher of the faith

whom exile could not keep

from proclaiming the truths

of Scripture and the Church,

whose pastoral zeal

called souls

to the blessed chamber

of our divine Lord Jesus Christ

that we might unite with Him

who united Himself with us

to draw us unto Heaven –

pray that the shepherds of the Church

shall be just so diligent

and faithful

as you have consistently been

in imparting the Word of God

to waiting ears and hearts,

that all might be nourished well

and so prepared

to meet our King and Bridegroom,

grace upon grace

overflowing in souls

led by the Spirit of Truth.

St. Joseph, Husband of Mary (March 19)

O righteous man called by God

to be foster-father of His only Son

and protector of His Mother,

you who were obedient to the Spirit,

who took Jesus by the hand

and led Him from the temple

in Jerusalem

to the home in Nazareth

where Mary made a place for Him –

pray that we shall be built

into the house of Abraham,

the man of faith,

into the house of David, your father,

into the House the Holy Spirit builds

for the faithful even this day,

where our Mother waits for us

with you and all the saints;

pray that we too shall hear the words

spoken over you by the Lord:

"Well done, good and faithful servant;

enter into the joy of your Master."

Pray we shall be righteous

as you.

Prayers to the Saints

St. Turibius de Mogrovejo (March 23)

O missionary shepherd

whose love for the truth

was a love for Christ

and a desire for your flock

to know Him

and the way to glorify God,

you who gave yourself

for the Truth that is Christ

and for His Church on earth,

through whom He teaches all men

and brings them into His fold —

may we, too, lay down our lives

and work as hard as you have done

in the Name of Jesus,

that all our lives

and the lives of all His flock

might be in accord

with the will of the Lord

and faithful to the Mother

He has left for our care;

let all that is not of God

be cast from our midst

by the Spirit of Truth this day.

Annunciation (March 25)

O chosen one of the Lord,

how well you answered His call,

giving yourself entirely

to the angel's word

and so conceiving in your womb

the salvation of the world –

pray, O Spouse of the Holy Spirit,

that His voice might inspire in us

your same commitment to the Word of God

and its working in our lives;

pray the Son be conceived in us as well

that we too might serve

to bring His salvation forth

into the light of this day.

How shall we give ourselves

completely to the Lord

without your prayers, dear Mother,

without your blessed intercession…?

O pray we shall follow in your wake

and add our 'yes' to your own,

that the Lord may indeed work in us,

that He might make His home in us

and we come to our home in Heaven.

Prayers to the Saints

APRIL

Prayers to the Saints

St. Francis of Paola (April 2)

O little one,

holy and true,

who wanted no more

than to leave the world

that you might draw closer

to Christ

but who was followed by the world

and called to teach the world

of the way of holiness

in our blessed Lord —

pray we shall follow His path

of Passion and death,

death to self

and all animosity, all hatred,

finding thereby His peace,

peace in His Spirit

and light.

O that we might be sanctified!

our hearts converted to God,

following your example,

which leads to the Cross

and so the resurrection

of our humble Jesus.

St. Isidore (April 4)

O learned man

whose wisdom remained

not only in the mind

but found practice

in the Church of God,

you who read and studied Scripture

not just for its own sake

but that the Word might be implemented

amongst your flock —

pray we too might live

with the Word of God,

that we too might share

the light He would impart

to every soul.

Pray God's grace

touch our innermost minds,

that the understanding our ear receives

will penetrate to our heart;

and pray, dear shepherd,

that God's Word permeate

His Church as a whole,

led by servants as learned as you

in the way of love and truth.

Prayers to the Saints

St. Vincent Ferrer (April 5)

O great preacher

who taught so well

the love of God

and the precepts of the Church,

who worked with such zeal

to repair the breach

within the Church

in a time of corruption —

pray that now the Word

may again go forth

to the ends of the earth,

that all might hear

the voice of the Spirit

speaking in their hearts

and turn resolutely

from their sins

to the grace of the Lord;

and pray, too,

there will be priests

to preach God's Word

with that same loving zeal

you had for the Church

and every soul.

St. John Baptist de la Salle (April 7)

O good teacher

of the poor boys in your care,

minister of the Lord

to those most in need,

with what humble affection

you carried out your work

in educating souls

in the Gospel of Christ

and guiding others to do the same —

pray that we, too,

shall give ourselves in sacrificial silence

to the call the Lord has placed

upon our souls,

and especially that teachers

of the young and disadvantaged

will find grace and strength

from our Lord

to carry out in truth and love

their work for Christ and His Church.

May the Temple of God

be built up on this earth

in all poor souls

washed in Christ's blood.

Prayers to the Saints

St. Stanislaus (April 11)

O soldier of Christ

who stood with courage

against the powers of this world,

leading the troops in your charge

even unto death —

pray that we may remain

loyal to our call,

faithful to the Lord

even unto our own death,

standing strong and tall

against the assaults of the world

and the devil

and forming those entrusted to us

in the ways of God

as you, dear shepherd,

have bravely done.

Let us not be afraid

to shed our blood for the truth,

to suffer persecution

in order to light the way

that leads to life,

the life that is Christ,

who strengthens us with the armor of God.

St. Martin I (April 13)

O martyred Father

of the Church,

you laid down your life

to save her from the enemy,

to preserve her in the truth

of orthodox faith;

unmindful of the humiliation

and exile you bore

at the hands of the king

of this world,

you died that all might know

the Christ

in His divinity and humanity —

pray we shall indeed be saved

from all temptation

to turn from the faith,

and so find our way

to the kingdom

where now you dwell

with the Lord and all His holy angels.

May our leaders be as strong as you

and we follow them loyally

in the Name of our Redeemer.

Prayers to the Saints

St. Anselm (April 21)

O sublime teacher

and defender of the Church

and her freedom,

the joy of Heaven

you sought

in your spiritual life,

and for the autonomy of Mother Church

you fought

in your call as shepherd —

pray that we

who remain so blind

to the presence of God

will have our eyes opened

and draw closer

to Him who is our life,

in whose light

we alone find peace;

and pray, too,

that we shall fulfill our call

as disciples of truth

and defend with your same strength

the life of our Mother,

despite the persecutions that come.

April

St. George (April 23)

O courageous soldier

in the army of our Lord,

you gave up the ranks

of this passing world

for the kingdom

wrought by Jesus Christ,

dying willingly

for such a just cause

and showing us the path

we must tread

to be found worthy

to stand with our God –

pray that we may be strengthened

in the battle of earthly life,

that our weak limbs

may not be disjointed,

that we might not tremble in fear

at the threats of the mighty

but take our refuge

in the Almighty

and fight for Him who fights for us

until we are wrapped in His arms,

until we cling to His breast.

Prayers to the Saints

St. Adalbert (April 23)

O persecuted shepherd

whose flock repeatedly drove you

from their midst

but who accomplished

great work of conversion

among them…

to these indignant souls

you repeatedly returned,

ever spreading Christ's net further –

pray for us, apostle to nations,

that in God's Church today

His Word may go boldly forth

to convert hearts

so hardened by sin,

that the acquired ignorance

of peoples returning to paganism

will be thoroughly dispelled

by truth.

Forth let all souls journey,

humbly proclaiming the Gospel

till all have heard and understood

the glory to which they are called

by our Savior.

April

St. Fidelis of Sigmaringen (April 24)

O charitable and zealous soul

who gave your life

that others might know

the true and abiding Catholic faith,

you who cared for the sick and the dying,

those who were ailing in body

and diseased in spirit —

how shall we learn

to sacrifice all as you have done,

to stand in the face of opposition

and speak the truth

though those we would help

would devour us instead

of listening to the words

come from the Savior's mouth?

Penance and prayer

are so far from us this day,

and who really cares

to show others Christ's way?

Pray this ship shall be strengthened

by holy souls

eager for the salvation of all

and confirmed in the truth and love of the Spirit.

Prayers to the Saints

St. Mark (April 25)

O proclaimer of the Word of God,

we know of our Lord

who suffered and died

that we might rise with Him

on the third day

because the Spirit inspired you

to tell us of this Good News.

Faithful you were to the Lord

and to His blessed apostles,

and so became an apostle yourself,

carrying the Gospel

to men of every nation —

pray that the Word

which you have served

to impart to us

may be remembered

and cherished in the hearts

of all believers,

and that we, too, shall work,

inspired by the Spirit,

to build up the Body of Christ,

making it ready for His return

to dwell with us forever.

April

St. Peter Chanel (April 28)

O great missionary,

you served to convert

a land and a people

that had never heard

of our blessed Savior,

and though killed for your work,

you loved those to whom you were sent

and toiled tirelessly

for their salvation —

pray the same kind heart you showed

we shall also know

in serving souls

placed into our care;

and pray the Name of our Lord

shall go forth in freedom

to the very ends of the earth

this day.

What are our lives

compared with the service of Christ

and the salvation of souls

in faith in His Name?

Let us live with your same zeal

the love that is Jesus and His Cross.

Prayers to the Saints

St. Louis Mary de Montfort (April 28)

O apostle of Mary

and so of our Lord Jesus Christ,

to the Lord you drew souls

through devotion to His Mother.

How perfectly you have spoken

of this grace upon the Virgin

and the role she plays

in the salvation of the world —

pray this day

that her sweet protection

and most blessed intercession

will be with all the children

who turn in faith to the one

chosen by the Father

to be Mother of His Son.

May this Spouse of the Spirit

lead us into God's presence

where with you

and all the heavenly saints

we shall find ourselves one

with the Most Holy Trinity

and sing forever the praises

of our Lord and God.

St. Catherine of Siena (April 29)

O wise and holy virgin

whose love for God

was matched by a great love

for the Church

and a great desire

to see her pure and holy

as He...

peace you brought to peoples

and to Mother Church,

for peace you held

within your blessed soul,

held as you were

in the hand of God –

pray the light of the Lord

will be shed upon His Church

and all souls

this day,

and that reconciliation shall come

and we stand as one

in that surpassing light

and peace of the Trinity.

May holiness be all men's desire,

to live in accord with the will of God.

Prayers to the Saints

St. Pius V (April 30)

O Shepherd of the Church

who led her through

a difficult time,

seeing to her reform

in faith and morals,

in teaching and prayer,

that the foundation once established

by the Lord Jesus Christ

might be confirmed

and strengthened,

kept from decay –

pray this day, too,

Mother Church will be blessed

by the nourishing food

of the Spirit,

that she might be fed

at the Lord's table

and all might be encouraged to enter

the gates of Heaven

she guards and opens

to all souls in communion

with the Savior and His way…

May Peter lead us unto His Day.

MAY

Prayers to the Saints

St. Joseph the Worker (May 1)

O humble laborer in God's House

who served to build up His Temple

by the sweat of your brow

and your careful concern

to follow His will —

pray that we shall embody

the same obedience

to the Word of God

and His call to our souls,

that we too will consecrate ourselves

and our daily labor

to service of the Lord

and the upbuilding of His Church,

and that we, too,

might be built into the House

wherein He makes

His eternal dwelling.

We are but poor creatures,

simple and weak;

pray the Lord our God

and His Son for whom you cared

will bless us with your dignity,

O righteous man of God.

St. Athanasius (May 2)

O defender of the faith

in the divinity of Christ,

bulwark of the Church

of the One

who is true God and true Man,

upholder of the way

in the face of all persecutions –

pray that the shepherds of the Church

will today be so staunch in the faith,

never afraid to defend the truth

from attacks from within

and outside her walls.

So many souls

are led so astray

by the teaching of false prophets;

pray indeed that the Lord

will raise up leaders,

prophets of His true teaching,

of His narrow way,

which leads through the body He assumed,

the death He took upon Himself

for our sins,

to His divine presence in Heaven.

Prayers to the Saints

Sts. Philip and James
(May 3)

O holy apostles of the Lord

upon whom the Church is established,

your words go out to the ends of the earth,

bringing the Gospel to all nations.

You who were near

to Jesus Himself,

who were with Him all the time

He walked among us…

there is no greater witness

to the way and the truth and the life

of our God, our Savior –

please pray for the Church in the world

this day,

that it shall be led by the Spirit of Truth

and we shall all be as brothers of the Lord,

living in His love

and revealing the Father.

As you have performed the works of the Son,

so let us join in the work of redemption,

that all the earth will come to see

that Jesus is in the Father

and we are made one in Him.

St. Damien de Veuster (May 10)

O leper with the lepers,

you united yourself

so thoroughly

with those you served

that you became one of them,

one of the frightful and rejected souls

abandoned by the world

but redeemed by the blood of Christ

through your intercession.

To them you brought the consolation

of government support

and the love of the Lord,

and so, many were inspired

to drag themselves

into your chapel –

pray we join them there,

listening attentively to the Word of salvation

and finding healing for the disease

that eats away at our souls;

help us to embrace the cross

the Lord provides

to lead us on the narrow way

to Heaven.

Prayers to the Saints

Sts. Nereus and Achilleus
(May 12)

O brave soldiers,

the world could not take

Christ from your hearts;

though it tried to expunge Him

from the army in which you served,

your allegiance to the holy One of Israel,

our Lord and God,

remained firm,

and so death you preferred

to life without Jesus —

pray for us who are so weak in faith,

that our stale complacency

might be invigorated

by the blood of our Savior,

the blood you yourselves shed

as you filled up what was lacking

in the sufferings of Christ.

Pray we shall not turn

from the sacrifice to which the Lord calls us

but embrace with joy

the cross we must bear,

and which bears us unto Heaven.

St. Pancras (May 12)

O child of courage,

though but a boy

you gave your life

as the strongest of men,

proving thus your love for Christ,

a love that steels souls

even in the face of death,

even in the youthful breast –

if but a young child like yourself

could die so freely for the faith

and show the face of Jesus

to the whole world,

how much more should we,

so graced by the Lord

with years of devotion,

be ready to give

for the Name of God?

Pray your innocence

may renew our hearts

and your strength

fortify our commitment

to give our lives for Christ

and His Church.

Prayers to the Saints

Our Lady of Fatima (May 13)

O marvelous Wonder,

O Lady who shines

like the sun,

who brings the Light

into our midst

and calls us to repentance

that we might be saved,

that the whole world

might turn to the Lord

and be preserved

from destruction…

you come at the end of the age

to lead us back to your Son

before He comes again

and finally –

pray we shall hear and heed

your warning to our souls

and, with the faith of the children

whose eyes beheld you,

offer ourselves

in union with the Cross of Jesus

for the salvation of all

and the renewal of the Church and the world.

St. Matthias (May 14)

O chosen apostle,

destined to serve the Church

as witness to the resurrection

of our Lord Jesus Christ,

you who walked with Him

from the beginning

even until He was taken

from our sight

yet were not appointed by the Spirit

as one of the Twelve

until a place was made desolate

by the traitorous one –

pray that the call upon the soul

of all God's children

will be fulfilled

according to His will

and we all shall come to be

witnesses to Jesus

and His eternal glory

wrought in our midst

by the power of the Holy Spirit.

Let none shy away from the Lord

but assume their rightful place in His presence.

Prayers to the Saints

St. Isidore the Farmer (May 15)

O farmer of God's green earth

who cultivated the faith

even as you cultivated the ground,

whose simple and humble life

should serve as inspiration

to all toiling on this plane –

pray that we shall follow your example,

sharing our food with the hungry

as we work for the salvation of souls.

Pray that all the work we do

will bear fruit in God's kingdom,

that with you and your wife

we may be found worthy

of those blessed words

come from our Savior's mouth:

"Well done, good and faithful servant.

Enter into your Master's joy."

Pray according to your own blessing

from the Lord

that this earth He has given us

to care for

may be saved from the greedy hands of corrupted man

and serve as source of nourishment for all.

St. John I (May 18)

O faithful Shepherd

who laid down your life

for the sake of true teaching,

who was killed by one

set against God's Word...

though deprived of food

and so of this life,

you were given instead

the life of Heaven

and serve as a holy example

of what should be sacrificed

for love of truth and right —

pray that the flock

shepherded this day by the apostles

will be led by the same loyalty,

led by genuine pastors

whose love for the sheep

would lead them to lay down their lives

that the Church might be blessed

by a radiant faith

which shines the light of Christ

even to the ends

of this dying earth.

Prayers to the Saints

St. Bernardine of Siena (May 20)

O apostle of the holy Name of Jesus

who proclaimed God's loving mercy

to those in darkness

that the light of faith

might save souls

and make them children

of the light of Christ,

radiating His splendor,

the splendor of truth,

to the ends of the earth —

where is such zeal today,

where apostles

with the preaching of Paul;

and so, how shall souls be saved,

how shall false beliefs flee,

infidelity be consumed

and the truth appear as a great candle

lighting the whole world with its brilliant flame,

if you do not intercede?

Pray that we may not lack

knowledge of and devotion to Jesus,

that His Name shall not be suppressed

but preached without cease to waiting hearts.

St. Christopher Magallanes and Companions
(May 21)

O sacrificial sheep,

priests of the Lord

who offered your lives

even as you offered Mass,

in union with Christ and His Church

for the sake of your homeland:

you prayed for its peace

even as violence was done to you;

you celebrated the Mass

and baptized your flock

even when it became a crime,

even when it cost your lives —

such union with Christ

pray all souls,

and especially our priests,

shall know to the depths of their heart;

let none be afraid

to shed their blood

as one with His redemptive sacrifice.

The Cross pray we follow

where it leads,

despite the world's persecution.

Prayers to the Saints

St. Rita of Cascia (May 22)

O saint of the impossible

whose union with Christ

in His Passion and His glory

serves to grant favors

to those in great need,

you whose great thirst

to be one with our Bridegroom

brought the help of the saints yourself —

pray we poor souls

shall fulfill our vocation,

that through the din of this world

we shall hear and answer

the call of the Lord

and give ourselves in His service

in the manner He desires.

Pray our hearts be so set

on union with Him

that no obstacle shall stand in our way,

that all help we need

to find our path to Him

will be provided through your prayers.

How shall we come to dwell in Heaven?

Invoke God's blessing upon us.

St. Bede the Venerable (May 25)

O learned master

whose life itself was as a monastery,

consumed as you were

by study and teaching and writing

and prayer,

who till the very end

spoke the Name of the Lord

in all your words

and deeds —

pray that the incense of your life

will rise unto the throne of God

and intercede for us here below

who are so far from His presence,

from knowledge of His providence

and remembrance of His sacrifice.

How will we find ourselves

one with the Lord of Creation

and ascend to His glory

if you do not pray for us,

O blessed soul

so united to His will,

so held within His Hand

and breathing forth His Name?

Prayers to the Saints

St. Gregory VII (May 25)

O Shepherd and Father,

defender of the faith

and of holy Mother Church

against those who would rob her

of her freedom,

those who would rape her,

stealing away her purity,

those who would deny

her singleness in the sight of God

as the House which He has founded —

those who would destroy the faith

and bring to naught

the Church, our Mother,

and Peter, our Holy Father,

do not relent in their efforts…

and so we need still

your prayers and your courage

to aid us in standing strong

against the tide

the evil one stirs up in this world.

Pray indeed, O Father,

that all our shepherds and all God's people

will tirelessly defend the truth in love.

St. Mary Magdalene de´ Pazzi (May 25)

O humble soul

whom the Lord blessed

with mystical elevations

to His heavenly presence,

you who remained so faithful

through all trials

and encouraged others

to seek such perfection as well –

pray that this proud age

which leans so distinctly

from the truth,

from the love of God,

will be consumed as you were

by the Holy Spirit,

by desire for the Lord's overtaking

of our lives,

that all souls will turn

from the false gods at their hands,

idols that overshadow their spirits,

and toward the humility

known only in our Savior's blood.

Only in Him is life eternal;

pray all souls will come to His love.

Prayers to the Saints

St. Philip Neri (May 26)

O priest of joy

whose song of service

rises unto the Lord

until this day,

whose delight in sacrifice

inspires others

to give themselves in freedom

to the work of Christ —

pray all God's priests

and people

will give themselves so completely

in the love of the only Son

that indeed a holy song

might rise unto the heavens

until He returns from there

to carry us home forever.

May the Lord's healing graces

be poured forth

through your generous intercession

that all souls might be prepared

to unite with their Creator and Redeemer,

with the Spirit who inspires the Church

even here with His glorious presence.

St. Augustine of Canterbury (May 27)

O converter of peoples,

called from the quiet

of cloister walls

you went obediently over seas

to preach to the souls

to whom you were sent,

and the Lord worked

through your obedience,

spoke through the words

you uttered to the nations…

and so the light of holy faith

banished the darkness of error

and souls indeed were gathered

into Christ's fold –

pray, O shepherd,

obedience shall be ours, too,

and that all whom the Father

would hold unto His breast

shall come indeed to that sacred place

and so find their rest.

May God's will be accomplished

in His Church

and we bear fruit in His Name.

St. Paul VI (May 29)

O lover of the Church

for whom you offered your life,

defending the saving truths of the faith

against the evil tide

engulfing humanity,

proclaiming the Gospel of Christ

and the light of the Lord

to the ends of a desolate world

drowning in a thousand false notions

of love

as man makes himself God

and so knows only emptiness

inside —

pray that we will extricate ourselves

from the embrace

of the culture of death

and find a civilization of love;

pray especially the smoke of Satan

will be blown by the Spirit

from this House you love

that She may be evangelized anew

and come to contemplate

the glory of God.

Visitation (May 31)

O Mother of our Lord,

who are we

that you should visit us?

Over hills you came

to see your cousin Elizabeth

and the child she conceived

so miraculously;

to her you brought the Child

who brings us all salvation.

Yes, to us all you bring Jesus…

all holy souls you visit with His grace.

John the Baptist proclaims this Savior

whom he has known first

in your voice,

and all hearts leap up

at your approach;

for the Lord is with you,

even in your blessed womb:

How blessed *is* this fruit you bear!

Visit us this day, dear Mother,

with Jesus our Redeemer,

that even this day

we may rejoice in His Name.

Prayers to the Saints

Mary, Mother of the Church
(Monday after Pentecost Sunday)

O Holy Tabernacle,

preeminent member and model of the Church

to whom you gave birth...

as you are Mother of the Head,

so, too, Mother of the Body,

of all those redeemed

by the Blood of your Son,

with whom you shared such intimate union —

pray that we be made fruitful

by your intercession,

children of the Lord Most High

and your children,

conceived of the Spirit that overshadowed you

and for whom you waited

with the apostles in the upper room.

Pray we make our home in you

as in the Church

born from the side of Jesus

pierced upon the Cross

beneath which you stood.

Dear Mother, pray we follow you

into glory.

May

Immaculate Heart of Mary
(Saturday following the 2ⁿᵈ Sunday after Pentecost)

O Sanctuary of the Father,

Temple of the Holy Spirit,

Mother of the Son of God

who carried Him in your womb

and contemplated Him

in your heart –

how shall we find Jesus

within us;

how shall we become

the temples of the Spirit

the Lord calls us all to be

if you do not pray for us,

if we are not formed

in your womb,

in the love

with which you are blessed?

Hold us in your soul, dear Mother,

that our spirits might join with your own

and we might thus

become one

with our Lord and brother.

In us also let Him make His home.

Prayers to the Saints

JUNE

Prayers to the Saints

St. Justin (June 1)

O prophet of the Lord

who spoke in His defense

even before the bench of death,

who professed the wisdom of the Cross

over the intelligence of our race

and all the ideas

it could conceive,

who chose true worship

of the One God

even over life itself

and taught us also

His way in His Church —

pray we shall merit with you

the name of Christian,

the Name above every other name,

upon our lips and hearts,

that we shall follow in His steps

seeking always the truth

and His love;

pray we shall worship Him

who deserves all worship and praise

and serve Him and His Church

even with our last breath on this earth.

Sts. Marcellinus and Peter
(June 2)

O blessed martyrs for the Lord,

in your catacombs the faith flourished,

upon your tomb the Church was built...

your blood is the seed

planted in the ground

that has caused the growth

of the tree of life;

joining in the sacrifice of Christ,

His great joy you knew –

pray that such grace

will be known to us this day,

that we will give ourselves in faith to the Holy One

by whom we are saved

and so find union with Him in Heaven.

How far His consolation is

from our souls this day,

for how little love we show:

have our hearts not become

as a tomb?

Though cold and lifeless,

by your prayers

may our faith flourish once more, dear saints.

Prayers to the Saints

St. Charles Lwanga and Companions
(June 3)

O modern martyrs for Christ

who gave your lives even as the early Christians,

under torture by the emperor,

who remained steadfast

as these

despite sword or fire

come by the power of the king...

a new age indeed you ushered in,

one of mighty suffering,

a time for the blood to mount up on this earth —

pray, brothers in the faith,

that your sacrifice not be in vain,

that we shall join you in loyal service

and so find the Church blessed

with new growth in the Spirit.

Though new to the faith yourselves

when you bled and died for the Word,

deeply was your foundation laid,

unshaken by the threats of the mighty.

Should we not be the same;

should we not follow in your way,

we who profess to love the Lord?

St. Boniface (June 5)

O apostle of the faith

called out from monastery walls

to travel into the world,

laboring and suffering

even to the shedding of blood

as you steered Christ's ship

pounded by waves

but kept on course,

spreading out upon the face of the earth

by the sacrifice of shepherds

like yourself —

pray the bishops of today

will unceasingly teach the faith,

defending the Church from all assaults,

never silent in the face of danger,

never turning from their call

but preaching the Gospel

in season and out of season

that in all seasons

Christ's flock might increase

and be strengthened.

Let us rather die

than give in to the impending darkness.

Prayers to the Saints

St. Norbert (June 6)

O preacher of the Word of God

and model of the Gospel,

you embraced poverty and penance

in accord with the way of Christ

and His teaching

and called your brothers

to do the same,

that the Church might be renewed,

that she might be holy

even as the Father is holy —

pray all souls

might indeed find holiness of life

even as within

cloister walls;

pray all might embrace

the poverty of Christ,

living the faith pronounced

in sacred Scripture.

And pray that they may be led

along this narrow path

to the kingdom of the Lord

by faithful priests and bishops,

shepherds like yourself.

St. Ephrem (June 9)

O harp of the Holy Spirit

whose song rose up to Jesus

and in honor of the Virgin Mary,

whose heart was set on Heaven

and the eternal light therein,

and who served so well to defend the faith

when from contemplation you came —

pray we too shall have a song

dedicated wholly to the Lord

welling up in hearts

set on His presence,

on the kingdom that passes not away;

and pray, too, the teaching of the Church

shall always be true,

shall always be rooted

in the Spirit,

expressive of the love of God.

What is this world as it passes away,

and who are we apart from God

and His House?

O how we long for Heaven!

Pray, dear brother, with our Blessed Mother,

that we shall come to dwell where you are.

Prayers to the Saints

St. Barnabas (June 11)

O son of encouragement

and of consolation in the Holy Spirit,

you who were filled with faith

and lived that faith for the Lord,

giving up all things to bring His Name forth

to the ends of the earth,

calling all souls

and confirming them in the truth

by the authority of the risen Son —

whose footsteps go forth today

as did yours

upon the birth of the Church;

what souls are so blessed

to be set apart by the Spirit

to perform His works

in this dying world,

to bring His light

to those who sit in darkness?

Pray the Lord shall indeed

send out laborers into His vineyard

and they shall with the same faith

be an encouragement to all,

a consolation to Christian souls.

St. Anthony of Padua (June 13)

O gentle preacher of the Word,

the fire of the Holy Spirit

upon your soul

for the conversion of heretics

and the leading of all

to God —

hold us in your arms

even as the infant Jesus

who appeared to you

along the way,

and pray that the Word

may be instilled in our hearts

even as it was in your own,

that we shall never go astray

but always have the consolation

of the Spirit of God

and His love and innocence

to lead us through this life

till we find ourselves

at home in the Father's arms,

where you dwell in peace

with all His blessed saints.

Pray for us, our teacher and brother, this day.

Prayers to the Saints

St. Romuald (June 19)

O sign of perfect solitude

who heeded so well

the Lord's command

to enter into your closet

in order to pray,

whose great measure of self-denial

led you to the peak of contemplation

in God's holy presence,

whose only desire

was that souls might draw close

to Him —

pray all who seek the Lord

may approach Him with a whole heart,

a heart set on Him alone,

that in such perfect devotion

all might find Him present

in their souls, in their spirits,

and be elevated in their lowliness

to His indescribable divine love,

to His peace which passes

all our understanding

but draws us ever closer

to His wounded side.

St. Aloysius Gonzaga (June 21)

O patron of youth

whose innocence was unsurpassed,

whose desire to give yourself

to the Lord

in poverty and purity

led you to relinquish

your wealth in this world

at a tender age

that you might embrace Jesus

fully —

pray for the youth of our day

and the child in each of our souls,

that all might turn away

from the temptations which surround

and threaten to enter and enslave;

let all turn toward

the love of the Lord

and His heavenly call,

a call to a kingdom

that surpasses everything of this earth

and brings the joy

known only in breathing and speaking

His holy Name.

Prayers to the Saints

St. Paulinus of Nola (June 22)

O lover of poverty

who gave up great wealth

to find her abiding

within the walls of your heart,

a heart which turned thus

to God's people

and the shepherding of them

with great care —

pray that we too may hear

and come to realize in our lives

the call of our Lord

to give up all things

for the sake of the kingdom,

to be attached to nothing

but service of the poor,

service of God Himself

in the humble of this earth;

pray that like you

we may have the heart of a shepherd,

of a laborer in Jesus' vineyard,

united in the Spirit

with all God's children

with whom we share His Heaven.

Sts. John Fisher and Thomas More
(June 22)

O kings of martyrdom

who indeed laid down

your very lives

rather than heed the dictates

of an evil emperor,

whose loyalty to the Lord

and the Church He established

stands unparalleled,

your defense of the faith

and conscience

written in the blood you shed —

pray that the mediocrity,

the utter inability to stand for truth

in this relativist age,

will be defeated

by souls founded firmly

in the Spirit of Christ

and in the Cross

He offers forth

for our salvation.

Pray for leaders of Church and State

to embrace your singular devotion.

Prayers to the Saints

Nativity of St. John the Baptist (June 24)

O greatest of men born of woman,

before you were formed in the womb

the Lord called you;

while still in this cave

you leapt for joy

at His presence come to you...

a sharp, two-edged sword He made you

to hail the coming Messiah,

the Light in our midst,

the New Covenant born of the Old —

how shall we humble ourselves

as you have done;

how shall our call be realized

in flesh and blood

as was your own?

Pray, dear brother,

that from darkness we be taken,

from blindness and inability to speak

we be rescued,

that the Word among us

we may know

and raise our voices

to proclaim His salvation to all.

St. Cyril of Alexandria (June 27)

O great defender of the Mother of God

and of the faith itself,

courageously you declared

that Jesus is God indeed,

become Man in Mary His Mother;

this you made plain for all to see,

O shepherd of the people of God,

that truth might reign

and the Virgin might find

her proper place among us —

pray, O brave teacher,

that we shall not be afraid

to proclaim the truths

inscribed by the Spirit

upon the heart of the Church

and in her inspired writings;

and may indeed our Mother,

the Mother of Jesus,

the Mother of God,

be recognized for her preeminence

amongst the saints,

that the Word of the Lord might be fulfilled

and all generations call her blessed.

Prayers to the Saints

St. Irenaeus (June 28)

O great teacher of the Catholic faith

who served to set a foundation

upon which she could grow

in peace and in truth,

in the Spirit of God,

you who valiantly defended her

against attacks of heresy

and shed your blood

in the battle —

pray we shall find shepherds today

to explicate the faith of the apostles

as clearly

and loyally

as you have done,

that none shall be led astray

into false doctrine

by whim and fancy,

by pride and envy,

but drink rather the pure milk

of our Mother

and of the one true God.

To vision of the Father let us come

by revelation of His only-begotten Son.

Sts. Peter and Paul
(June 29)

O most blessed apostles of the Lord
upon whom the Church is founded
and the faith goes forth,
in you we cannot be shaken
and the Lord's reign extends
to the ends of the earth —
pray we always take refuge
in His House
and in the teaching of His mouth.
It is you who preserve
the authenticity of the faith;
through you we may be assured
the Spirit of God is with us,
leading us out of the dark prison
of this world
along the narrow path
to Heaven.
Pray the chains fall from our hands
and we heed the angel's command,
remaining faithful to the end,
pouring out our lives like a libation.
Feed the poor sheep in your care.

Prayers to the Saints

First Martyrs of the Holy Roman Church
(June 30)

O first of souls to shed blood,

whose sacrifice began the great persecution,

you indeed handed your bodies over

to torture,

to the mad king of this dark world,

but everlasting reward

you have gained

for yourselves and for the Church;

your robes washed clean

in the blood of the Lamb,

you served to nourish the growth

of the people of God —

pray your holy offering

shall always be remembered,

that the Church in this day

and in all days

may be blessed by your witness

of faith,

that you might light our path to Heaven

until our crucified Lord returns again

to gather all of faith and courage

into His redeeming arms.

JULY

Prayers to the Saints

St. Junípero Serra (July 1)

O missionary of the New World

inspired to leave your classroom

and go forth to win souls for Christ,

despite continuous battles

with cold and hunger

and long journeys with an injured leg,

praying throughout the night

you persevered and stayed

with the thousands you baptized

into the fold of Mother Church,

bringing them not only the gift of faith

but better living conditions as well;

fighting ever against the military powers

that would have brought only slaughter,

you gained rights for these natives

in the missions of California –

pray we shall have

the same zeal for souls

that, thinking not of ourselves

and without concern for any suffering,

we may bear the image of our Lord

to the ends of the earth

so all might come to salvation.

St. Thomas (July 3)

O believing apostle

who declared the divinity of Jesus,

our Lord and our God,

all doubt disappears

in the light of your faith,

for we see with you

what is beyond all eyes —

pray for an increase

in our faltering faith,

that we shall indeed believe

though we do not see;

let it be as if we ourselves

have touched the nail marks

in His hands and feet

and placed our hands into His side.

So firmly let our faith be founded

that we shall reach out

to all mankind

and the truth of Christ

as the Son of God

will grow in all hearts

until that Day we see the Lord

with our own eyes.

Prayers to the Saints

St. Elizabeth of Portugal (July 5)

O reconciler of warring sons,

tranquility in the midst

of great disturbance,

though born of royal blood

and married to a king,

the Lord you preferred

to all the riches of this world,

and so His peace

became your own —

pray we, too, may keep our hearts

set upon that which passes not away

and the peace which passes understanding;

pray our prayers be deep as your own

and reflect the same tranquility,

that those in our own families

and those under our care,

all those whom we meet

and to whom we relate,

may find the Lord's peace

dwelling in us

with His divine charity

and so be reconciled to Him

and to one another.

St. Anthony Mary Zaccaria (July 5)

O child of the Apostle Paul,

follower in his steps,

preacher of the Word

he proclaimed so completely

with his very life,

you who desired so

to bear the fruit of love in patience,

to share in the hardships of the apostles

as well as in their glory,

and led your fellow ordained

zealously to desire the same —

pray there shall be reform

in this day among our priests

and among the people of God,

that all will so zealously follow

the teaching and way of the Apostle,

which is, of course, the way of Christ:

to die, to lay down our lives,

to suffer indignation

and pray for our enemies,

all the while calling souls

to the Lord's undying love,

to His saving blood.

Prayers to the Saints

St. Maria Goretti (July 6)

O perpetual virgin

who defended your purity

even with your life

and so earned the crown

of martyrdom

at a tender age...

O bride of Christ

who prayed even for your murderer

and so served to inspire

his conversion —

pray for us, too, dear child;

pray the lust and violence

so prevalent in this world of sin,

and in our own hearts,

be purged from our midst

that we, too, might turn

to Jesus

and find the purity

He offers.

O pray innocence and chastity

overtake this age

and all souls stand

in the light of Christ.

St. Augustine Zhao Rong and Companions (July 9)

O righteous band of martyrs

united by faith in Christ and His Church

in a nation of religious oppression:

children and grandparents,

workers and teachers,

lay and ordained,

native and foreign-born…

all as one you gave your lives,

led by your convictions –

pray the Word of the Lord

come to a land so cold

to conversion,

to the love and worship

of Jesus, all men's Savior.

Pray the Holy Spirit

fall like purging and redeeming fire

upon every soul

in the country where you

so honorably died;

pray His power spread

and bring renewal

upon the face of all the earth.

Prayers to the Saints

St. Benedict (July 11)

O monastic father

who led the way into the desert

where the Lord speaks to men's hearts,

where He calls souls to perfect worship,

putting Christ before all else

and treating others as He Himself...

O you who prayed most perfectly,

you who knew God so intimately —

pray that our distracted minds

will somehow be conformed

to listening for His voice

and answering His call

to serve Him with all our lives.

Help us, dear brother,

dear father in the faith,

to find our dwelling place

in the kingdom,

to live so completely

according to God's Word,

that with great fervor,

with overflowing love,

we may accomplish His will

and join you in His presence.

St. Henry (July 13)

O you who were king and emperor

yet set your sights

on the reign of Heaven

and the reform and upbuilding

of the Church on earth,

who dedicated yourself

to the Lord of all

and service of His apostles —

pray our cares and responsibilities

will not distract us

from remembrance

of our God and His mercy

but that we shall indeed

dedicate these

and all our lives

into the hands of our Savior,

that He might dispose of them and us

as He sees fit.

Pray our kingdom not be of this earth

but of Heaven

and that we shall make our home

at the foot of the throne

of the Almighty.

Prayers to the Saints

St. Kateri Tekakwitha (July 14)

O wise virgin

so willing to leave your people behind

to wed the only One

who could win your heart,

the Lord Jesus Christ,

you were not swayed

by punishment or persecution

to renounce Him whom you loved

but remained humble and diligent

in your chastity and poverty and penance,

sleeping on thorny mats

for your Bridegroom and your persecutors —

pray we too will be led into the desert,

into the wilderness where God speaks,

that we, too, might be espoused to Him

and wait patiently for His coming,

when all our scarred faces

will be transformed as yours by His glory.

Pray every tribe and tongue and nation

will come in innocence before the Lord

and so be adopted

as sons and daughters

of the great King.

St. Bonaventure (July 15)

O good doctor

who taught the way to God

by death to things outside the Cross,

by resting with Christ

in the tomb

that we might pass

from this world to the Father —

pray our passions

indeed be silenced

that the fire of God

will carry our soul

to Him who is beyond

the operations of our mind;

pray our surrender to Him

may be complete

and the Holy Spirit lead us

in loving flame

to the kingdom.

Where is the longing of our soul

for God,

and who will assist us on the journey?

Speak to our hearts this day, good teacher,

from your place in His radiant presence.

Prayers to the Saints

Our Lady of Mount Carmel (July 16)

O Mother of contemplation

who heard the Word of God

and kept it,

pondering its wonder

in your heart,

you who were so faithful

to His call

and remain ever in His presence —

how shall we know our Lord

if you do not pray for us,

if you do not intercede

for souls so blinded

by the distractions

and temptations

of a fallen world?

Our prayers are with you, dear Mother,

who pray as one with our dear Lord,

who are so one with Him

in body and soul,

who stand at His side this day

in the kingdom of Heaven…

There on His holy mountain

help us to make our home.

St. Camillus de Lellis (July 18)

O servant of the sick

whose compassionate heart

melted at the sight

of every suffering soul,

who constantly visited Christ

as He lay in hospital…

how deep was your charity,

how complete your love and dedication

to the poor —

pray that we too shall leave

the cares of the world behind

and have only concern

for serving Christ

and our fellow man;

pray the hard hearts of this age

will be saved by the Lord's grace

even as they look upon Him

in the face of those in need.

How shall we match your stature,

which was so like Jesus' own;

how shall we find perfect charity,

taking the Lord into our homes?

Pray our hearts be set on Him alone.

Prayers to the Saints

St. Apollinaris (July 20)

O suffering shepherd

severely persecuted

for your work of evangelization,

you ever continued to preach the faith

and convert multitudes

despite all the tortures

the ravenous beasts of this earth

could muster;

a true apostle you proved to be,

martyred even as Christ's Twelve —

how shall we find

a measure of your conviction,

of your persistence

in spreading the Gospel of the Lord?

Pray for us, blessed shepherd,

that we who are weak of will

and so fearful

of the slightest disturbance

to our comfort and ease

shall learn by God's grace

to give our lives

as freely as you

in the service of man's salvation.

St. Lawrence of Brindisi (July 21)

O great preacher of the Word of God,

you who were entrusted

with this angelic office

to bring light to Christian minds

and dispel the darkness

of sin and error —

pray all souls this day

may be blessed with hearing

the Word of God you spoke so well,

that all hearts might turn in faith

to the Lord

purged by its cleansing fire.

O blessed teacher,

pray men of every tongue

be told of the truth,

that all might live

by the Spirit of God

in grace,

that the renewal of the Church

and every soul

might be made complete

and the ranks of the New Jerusalem

be filled to overflowing.

Prayers to the Saints

St. Mary Magdalene (July 22)

O woman of great love

whose heart burned

with desire for the Lord,

whose soul thirsted for the living God…

the tears you cried

became the source

of the greatest joy

as from your sins the Christ released you,

as your eyes beheld

your blessed Teacher —

pray for us this day, O Mary,

that our hearts shall be set aflame

with faith and love

as we hear the news you bring us:

that our Lord is no longer in the tomb,

that He lives

and so we with Him,

that He is ascending to the Father

and we shall join Him there.

O pray His love

dispel the coldness of our hearts

that we shall be like you,

remaining with Him forever.

St. Bridget (July 23)

O seer of the Passion

of our Lord Jesus Christ,

of the scourges and the nails,

of the blows and mockery

He endured,

of the blood which covered

His face and all His skin...

O you who have witnessed

all His suffering

and sought so diligently

to share in it with Him —

pray that we who are so blind

to the pain and anguish

our Savior bore

under the weight of the Cross

we build by our sin

may by His grace

have our eyes opened,

and so turn from our own condemnation

to the blood of redemption

He has shed for our sakes

and take refuge in the penance

that leads all souls to the kingdom.

Prayers to the Saints

St. Sharbel Makhluf (July 24)

O solitary prayer,

alone with the Lord

in the Blessed Sacrament

you offered your life

for the salvation of souls;

in penance you lived,

and so a light shone

even from your tomb

to show the presence of Christ

and His miraculous powers

at work in the world —

pray all souls

seek perfection in prayer,

the perfection of being with Jesus,

of remaining always in His presence

with a heart of love

poured out for our fellow man.

Pray even now

for the salvation of all,

for what else matters

but that we come to dwell

with you in the light of our Lord,

adoring Him forever?

St. James (July 25)

O martyred apostle,

first to endure the death of Christ,

you have indeed drunk of His cup,

fully accepting the sacrifice

to which all are called,

and so blazed the path of service

for others to follow –

pray all God's children,

all those blessed to be called as sons,

as brothers of the Lord,

will have the courage and strength

that comes from the Spirit

to lay down their lives

as a ransom for many

and so find a place

beside our Savior Jesus

in His heavenly kingdom.

Pray the blood of Christ

in which you shared so intimately

pour upon His Church

and all souls be blessed

to drink thereof

unto the world's salvation.

Prayers to the Saints

Sts. Joachim and Anne (July 26)

O parents of the Virgin Mary,

grandparents of the Lord our God,

you who gave birth

to our Blessed Mother,

through whom we are blessed

for all ages…

O you through whom the promise to David

came to be fulfilled,

you whose virtues

found favor with the Lord,

you whom He chose

to bring forth His Mother

and the Mother of all the redeemed –

pray our posterity shall endure

even as your own,

that we shall bear fruit

even in our old age

and see our children's children

in a happy Jerusalem.

Pray we shall know the Virgin

as intimately as you

and so come to know our Lord

in the kingdom where He reigns.

St. Martha (July 29)

O servant of the Lord

who welcomed Him

into your home,

fulfilling all the duties

of hospitality,

and yet realized

as He taught

that it is He

who serves us poor creatures,

who is the resurrection and the life...

in whose House we make our home –

pray that even as we fulfill the duties

of our station in life

we too shall come to believe

Jesus is the Christ,

the Son of God

who comes to us

to serve us in His need,

allowing Himself to be fed by us

that He might feed our souls

with everlasting life,

with the Spirit that passes not away

with the body.

Prayers to the Saints

St. Peter Chrysologus (July 30)

O you of golden words,

of angelic tongue,

of sermons refined

seven times

by the Spirit of God...

O how you made present on earth

the invisible Creator

even as He was made for us

in the womb of the Virgin,

so tangible had His grace become

through the preaching the Lord inspired

in your soul —

pray we shall indeed be vivified

by the eternal grace of God,

by the gift of His becoming Man,

to become like Him,

heavenly spirits in His reign.

How could we comprehend such blessing;

how could such surpassing joy

these earthen vessels hold?

Let us come close to Christ our Savior,

close to Him as now you stand

in His radiant glory.

St. Ignatius of Loyola (July 31)

O strong and holy apostle,

soldier for the Lord Jesus

and defender of His Church,

you gathered together an army

to labor in mission fields,

to educate the masses,

to serve and die as loyal sons

of the Christ and His Pope —

teach us this day

to follow in the way of Jesus,

to meditate on His life

and be fruitful in His works.

Pray your own sons

and all the children of Mother Church

not waver in the faith

which sustains them on this earth

but that in all truth

Christ's disciples shall stand steadfast

and proclaim in strength the salvation

that comes only through Jesus

and the Vine He has planted,

through whose teaching and sacraments

His very Spirit and blood flow.

Prayers to the Saints

AUGUST

Prayers to the Saints

St. Alphonsus Liguori (August 1)

O patron of moral theologians

and servant of the poor,

how blessed was your loving wisdom,

your understanding of God

and His love for us,

made perfectly known

in His only Son

whom you loved so much

with His Mother and the Church,

and whom you call us all to love

through your blessed words —

pray the redeeming love

of Jesus our Savior

flow in all our veins,

that we might unite our wills

to the Father's

as perfectly as His only Son

and so be as encompassed by grace and love

as only He could be.

Pray indeed that we shall be saved,

that we will come to the Lord on our knees

and so find His presence filling us

unto eternity.

St. Eusebius of Vercelli (August 2)

O vigorous defender of the divinity of Christ,

you who suffered exile

for your work for the faith,

you who had a true shepherd's heart

and cared so deeply

for the priests and people

the Lord placed in your hands —

pray the shepherds of the Church today

will strive with your same selfless zeal

to bring the love of the Son of God

and the blessed demands of His call

to every soul in their care,

that the faith might increase

and be known in all its fullness

even to the ends of the earth.

Pray and weep, O steadfast apostle,

for all the members of Christ's holy flock,

that we shall be protected

from false and specious claims,

from wolves in sheep's clothing

who would enter and steal the faith

of this holy Catholic Church

founded by our Lord Jesus Christ.

Prayers to the Saints

St. Peter Julian Eymard (August 2)

O priest of the Blessed Sacrament,

you gave your life in sacrifice

at the altar of the Lord

and in all the trials of this earth;

you suffered all for Jesus

and desired only to bring souls,

all the children of God,

to receive Him and His grace

in the Sacrament of Communion,

in oneness with our Lord —

pray, O priest of Christ,

that our very lives

shall also be offered in sacrifice,

especially in the holy sacrifice

of the Mass

and in reception of His Body and Blood

in the Blessed Sacrament.

Pray particularly that our priests will know

the profound call upon their souls

to make Him present in this world

and be as inspired with holy devotion

as were you, dear saint.

Pray our hunger for His Presence increase.

St. John Mary Vianney (August 4)

O priest exemplar,

O preacher and confessor extraordinaire,

healer of souls

who by prayer and penance

was made holy unto God

and brought others

to that same holiness

before the Lord and Maker

of all poor souls —

pray indeed this day

that our hearts will be set on Heaven,

that our longing will be for the Lord,

and so that by prayer

we shall come to union with Him.

Pray all your fellow priests

will be filled with your same zeal

for the salvation of their flock

and so serve to bring them

to blessed union

with the God of all.

Pray the Lord send out holy priests

to labor in His vineyard

as diligently, as tirelessly, as you.

Prayers to the Saints

St. Sixtus II and Companions
(August 7)

O martyrs of the faith,

ordained by the Lord

to shed blood for His sake

and the sake of His Church,

to give witness to the glory of Christ

and so win the crown

of eternal life…

it is in your blood

and by your sacrifice

the Church has grown

and become strong —

pray it shall always stand firm

in confessing the faith

despite any threat

from the powers of this world;

pray every soul

shall give his life in joy

and so emerge victorious

in the spiritual combat.

Handed over to death

for Jesus' sake,

may we, too, come to eternal life.

St. Cajetan (August 7)

O reformer of the Church

and leader of her priests and people,

calling all to live the Gospel,

to give their hearts

in the service of Christ,

who alone can save men's souls —

pray that your love for the Lord

and His holy Church

will be known in all

the members of His Body,

and so that apostles will be sent forth

to preach and to heal

even this day.

Pray we shall be one

with Him who made us,

eating His Body and drinking His Blood

and living according to the Word

He speaks to our souls

through Mother Church

and all her faithful servants.

It is the Lord alone

who must be our concern;

pray we, too, shall walk in His footsteps.

Prayers to the Saints

St. Dominic (August 8)

O humble preacher

who walked in poverty

with Christ your King

and spoke in power

to destroy lie by truth,

you gathered men around you

to be bearers of the grace of God,

to be men of the Gospel

inspired by love divine –

pray we shall be taught well

the faith

and walk with you in Jesus' way,

that all we do

will be for the salvation of souls,

our lives even as our Savior's.

May His Word

and deep love for others

lead us in all our work on earth

that always and in all things

we may beseech the Lord

to be with all His brothers.

Pray our hearts be set on His will

and we serve as His apostles.

St. Teresa Benedicta of the Cross (August 9)

O sacrificial victim

seeking to bring peace

to a dark world,

you found your wisdom in love,

in the love of Christ

and in His Cross,

and died three times for His sake:

once in entering His Church,

once in taking His habit,

and once in laying down your life

at the hands of the enemies of His peace –

pray, O blessed teacher

and sister to all men,

that the death of this life

be something we shall not fear

but embrace with the same grace

with which the Lord blessed you.

Why should we hold

to the things of the earth

when Jesus waits to embrace us

in His loving arms

and carry us unto Heaven?

Pray we shall be ready to answer His call.

Prayers to the Saints

St. Lawrence (August 10)

O generous soul,

you gave your life freely

to the poor

and your death completely

to the Lord;

a grain of wheat fallen to the earth,

you have indeed produced much fruit,

so closely have you followed Christ –

pray for us miserable souls

who cannot seem to draw near

your thorough sacrifice,

made without fear of the fire

ignited by your torturers,

made in joy of uniting

your death to Jesus' own.

How shall we approach your love,

your blood so closely mingled

with that of our crucified Lord;

how shall we match your generosity

in serving His blessed call?

Pray we will find the courage

to give everything over to God

and know we are in His arms.

St. Clare (August 11)

O bride of Christ

whose poverty matched His own,

whose humility made Him known,

whose love indeed approached

His throne

and the embrace of His holy arms —

pray all souls will gaze into the mirror

that is our Lord

born in a manger,

dead upon a Cross,

risen unto Heaven.

Pray we shall be driven on

through the death we all must die,

through His marvelous poverty,

His wondrous humility,

to the indescribable delights

of those who remain at His side.

O that we might be poor as you were poor,

as He is poor

for the sake of every soul,

that we might come to embrace

His blessed sacrifice

and so know the glories of His kingdom.

Prayers to the Saints

St. Jane Frances de Chantal (August 12)

O tireless worker for the Lord

who when cut off from everything

dearest to you

gave yourself completely to God,

you who have shown the way

of the martyrdom of love,

of dying entirely to self

and serving our Savior

in the sick and the poor,

in whose guise He comes —

pray our lives shall not wallow

in mediocrity

or sin;

pray we shall have

the same thirst for love as you,

that by our love we may die

and so overcome death

to live forever

in the presence of our Redeemer.

Visit us this day in our weakness

that our hearts, too, might be strong

and our lives be laid down

in the blood of the only Son.

Sts. Pontian and Hippolytus
(August 13)

O brothers united in faith

and in offering the ultimate sacrifice

for the sake of that faith,

for the sake of God's Church —

pray nothing shall separate

Christ's brothers

one from another,

but that all members of His flock

and all those who lead His flock

will remain ever united

in His blood

under the See of Peter.

O pray that His Body

not be divided

but that it be healed,

made whole

by His Cross.

Into His arms

may we all offer

our lives

and so join our Lord

in His kingdom.

Prayers to the Saints

St. Maximilian Mary Kolbe (August 14)

O soldier of the Immaculate Virgin

and martyr for our Lord,

well you spread the fame

of the Mother of all graces,

calling all souls to repentance

that she might apply her Son's blood

to save the straying among us;

and well you heeded our Savior's call

to lay down your life for others —

pray this day we have such strength,

such conviction and determination

in serving our Lord and Lady,

in publishing the Good News

of salvation,

that by our dedication

we too may serve well upon this earth

in the army of the faithful,

also leading souls

through the Immaculate Heart of Mary

to the Sacred Heart of Jesus,

that peoples and nations may be converted

and so learn in turn to serve

the surpassing glory of God.

Assumption (August 15)

O glorious Virgin Mary,

preserved from sin

from the moment of your conception

and now raised with your Son unto Heaven,

blessed are you among women,

most blessed of all God's creatures;

kept from all corruption,

you His lowly servant

now reign with Jesus in His kingdom –

pray all generations will call you blessed

that all may indeed share in your blessing

and come by the grace of the Lord

to stand at His side

in the Father's presence.

Above the choirs of angels,

where poor mortal man is called

to take his place

in union with the immortal Godhead,

you precede us, O Immaculate Mother,

by virtue of your eternal union with the only Son.

Pray we shall truly follow you to perfection,

conquering death by the Cross

and entering the light of the Lord.

Prayers to the Saints

St. Stephen of Hungary (August 16)

O faithful king,

loyal son of Mother Church

and just ruler of your people,

in peace and piety,

humbly and honorably

you executed your duties,

never showing favor to anyone

but always respecting all

and maintaining above all the faith

and the Church which propagates

that faith in Christ —

where is true Christian profession today,

where those in positions of power

truly dedicated to right service

of the Lord and His people?

Do pray for us, dear king,

that others shall follow in your footsteps

as has your son

so that all shall become

faithful followers of our Lord

in whatever position He grants them.

Pray especially for leaders

whose hearts are set on love of God and holy Church.

St. John Eudes (August 19)

O priest of Jesus and Mary

so dedicated to the Hearts

of our Lord and Lady

and the formation of your fellow priests,

how well you preached

of our need to be one

with Christ our Head,

with what zeal you cared

for the poorest among us —

pray that priests and indeed all Christians

will have hearts and souls

beating and breathing as one

with the Lord,

in union with our Blessed Mother;

may all serve and glorify the Father

by using all their faculties

as if they were His alone.

O that we might indeed

belong to the Son of God

and be ruled by Him,

His own eternal life

coursing through our very veins,

His breath upon our tongue!

Prayers to the Saints

St. Bernard (August 20)

O great light of the Church

who by word and work

inspired your brothers

and so many others

to a life of virtue,

to peace and unity with one another

and an abiding love

for our Lord and His Mother —

teach us this day, O blessed preacher,

of the way in which Jesus calls us,

of the life and love God offers

if we but respond in kind

in our weak and limited manner.

To all souls in His holy Church

and throughout the world

you brought the Word of God,

you imparted the light of His wisdom;

please pray, dear father in the faith,

that our lives may be conformed

to the loving will of the Lord

and we become children of His light

and bearers of His Good News to the nations,

till we stand with you in His surpassing glory.

St. Pius X (August 21)

O simple priest

who became Shepherd

of the universal Church

and defended her with courage

against the errors of the age,

you did not waver before the powers

that would dilute the purity

of the teaching of our Mother

but stood strong against the tide

attempting to wash her away —

are we not yet threatened

by falsehood and sin

being held up as good,

and so do we not yet need

your spirit and your prayers?

Though the tide may be turning,

returning to the solid rock of faith,

yet certainly we need your help

to see the Spirit of Truth

regain and maintain

His place in this House.

Pray indeed all priests and people

be simple and true as children before God.

Prayers to the Saints

Queenship of Mary (August 22)

O Queen of Heaven and earth,

you radiate the glory of God,

for now you stand at His right Hand

in the heavenly kingdom.

Clothed with the sun,

the moon under your feet

and a crown of twelve stars

upon your head,

you give light to all souls

who thirst for the grace

our Lord and King

pours upon us through your intercession.

O how the angels rejoiced,

how the heavens rang with praise

when the Son led you into His presence

clothed in gold

to be forever His Bride!

O pray for us,

dearest Queen and Mother,

that we too shall be led in

among your maiden companions

to stand in God's glory forever.

Our cause we entrust to your Immaculate Heart.

St. Rose of Lima (August 23)

O penitential soul

whose eyes saw the Lord,

whose ears heard His voice

calling all to the Cross,

obediently you accepted

the afflictions that are necessary

to attain union with God

and His surpassing glory –

pray that fearful souls

like our own,

which turn in complaint

from every torment and trouble,

however small,

may be blessed with a measure

of your selfless devotion,

that the unfathomable treasure

of the Lord's grace

might be our own

as we endure,

and even desire as you,

the pains that pave the road to Heaven.

Then we shall know Christ even as you

and proclaim His glory to all creatures.

Prayers to the Saints

St. Bartholomew (August 24)

O apostle of the Lamb,

man without guile

led by love to the Lord,

you who declared Jesus Son of God

and King of Israel,

whose eyes of faith were illumined

by angels' wings –

pray we shall be found by the Christ

under our fig tree

in peace, in prayer,

and carry with you His holy Gospel

to the very ends of the earth.

With you as a foundation stone,

one of the Twelve,

may the Bride of the Lamb

be led to her Husband,

her heart burning with love

for Him alone;

her soul thirsting only for God's presence,

may her eyes be opened

to see her Lord.

To vision of Heaven pray we all come

by an angelic belief in the Son of Man.

St. Louis of France (August 25)

O loyal subject of the Lord

and of His Church on earth,

though a king

you did not exalt yourself

but listened rather

to the words of your Savior

and chose to serve Him,

doing His work in this world:

the poor you cared for,

your children you raised

in the teaching of Christ,

and for all those in your reign

you sought true justice

and maintained concern

for their spiritual welfare –

pray we poor souls

will emulate your desire

for penance and prayer,

and your faithful obedience

to God and Mother Church.

May we be blessed as your sons

to have your wisdom in our ears,

a wisdom reflective of Jesus' own.

Prayers to the Saints

St. Joseph Calasanz (August 25)

O guardian angel of poor children

who formed them in the image of Christ,

an education of body and soul

you provided those most in need,

those most impressionable

and thirsting for the Lord's care,

and led so many others

in this work for the least of our brothers —

pray we shall become fellow workers

with Jesus in the cause of truth

and teach with deep love,

the greatest patience,

and profound humility,

the souls He places in our hands.

May the desire to see all

attain eternal life

be that which most impels us

and especially those whose responsibility

is the formation of Christian youth,

that all men might rejoice at the straight paths

these walk to the kingdom.

Your zeal despite persecution

may we maintain in our call from the Lord.

St. Monica (August 27)

O tearful mother

whose persistent cries

for the soul of your son

were heard in time

by the Lord our God

and so led to his conversion,

to his becoming

not only a Catholic Christian

but a bishop and doctor of the Church,

a saint like yourself —

pray for the prayers of all mothers

who cry for their wayward sons;

pray indeed that all souls may turn

and come to know so deeply

the love of our Lord and God

and the blessing upon

His holy Catholic Church.

Pray that all who stray,

many as they are,

shall be raised from the death of sin

and come to the life of Heaven,

where you wait with your son

to welcome all his brothers.

Prayers to the Saints

St. Augustine (August 28)

O shepherd made anew

by Him who is within,

Him who made us all,

the Light above and beyond

every soul

who gave His life,

His flesh as food that we might live —

pray that the Lord and God of all

will break through our deafness

and dispel our blindness,

that He will breathe His fragrant Spirit

upon us

and we too will be created

anew,

saved by His grace from the sin

that has kept us from Him

and thirsting for the wisdom

which became your own,

with which you shepherded His people

apart from the things He created

to His very Beauty itself,

that all souls might rest in Him

who made them.

Martyrdom of St. John the Baptist (August 29)

O witness to the Truth,

to the Light that has come among us,

you gave your very life

and death

for the sake of Christ,

who redeemed us in His blood,

blood you shed with your Savior;

you who were a pillar of iron

against the whole land

and against its king,

you who stood so strong

against the lust of the world,

suffering its persecution so willingly,

fortified even in death

by the Lord and His promise —

how can our meager lives

measure up to your blessed sacrifice;

how can we who are so weak of knee

endure our exile so bravely?

Pray for us, O forerunner of the Christ

both in word and in the giving of your life,

that our blood may be joined to your own

and so to that of our holy Lord.

Prayers to the Saints

SEPTEMBER

Prayers to the Saints

St. Gregory the Great (September 3)

O great Shepherd,

watchman of the House of God

and protector of His flock,

though in the monastery you would have stayed,

when called to the Chair of Peter

you guided the Church well

through difficult times —

pray that as difficult days continue

a firm hand may continue to be found

at the helm of Mother Church.

O pray that the faith be strengthened,

that the Rock upon which this House is set

will remain unshakable

and its light, its wisdom,

serve ever as a beacon

calling straying souls

into the Lord's welcoming arms.

Humility and holiness

may all our leaders embody,

that by the Word of God on their tongues

and His wounds in their hands

all the poor of the earth

will be carried unto Heaven.

St. Teresa of Calcutta (September 5)

O lover of the poor

and of the unborn,

in whom you saw

the face of Christ,

by whom you held Him

close to your heart

and so comforted His thirst

for souls —

pray for us who are so blind

to the presence of Christ

in the least among us

or even in those

beside us.

Pray, dear Mother,

that we will hear their cry,

which is Jesus' cry

from the Cross,

and that we shall not fear

the darkness

as we enter beneath the shadow

of His loving arms,

where we shall find

true light.

Prayers to the Saints

Nativity of Mary (September 8)

O Virgin who bore the Son of God,

who became the divine dwelling place

for the Creator of us all,

should we not celebrate your birth

this day,

the blessing of the generation

of you who signal our salvation?

Pray for us, dear Mother,

pray for all your children,

all who would call themselves

sons of God

and brothers of our Lord Jesus Christ...

pray that all generations

will call you blessed,

that all will hail you

as Mother of our Savior

and glorify the Lord

who has filled you with His grace.

You are one of us, dear Virgin Mary,

one of the human creation,

yet in you God deigns to dwell;

pray we shall all be made worthy

to be such a temple for the Lord.

September

St. Peter Claver (September 9)

O slave to the slaves,

to those who came in chains

to the new world,

those whose dark skin

made them seem to eyes of flesh

less than men...

to you these were children of God,

souls to be saved by His love

and through His Church,

and so the thousands

baptized by your hands

celebrate your glorious sacrifice

this day in God's presence –

pray for us, dear brother,

that the shackles of racial prejudice,

the pride that exalts man above man,

shall fall from our hands,

our tongues and our hearts,

and that all of the Lord's holy people

will work so diligently

as you, His blessed slave,

for the care of the weakest among us

and the salvation of all souls.

Prayers to the Saints

Most Holy Name of Mary (September 12)

O Mary, sweetest of creatures,

whose name on our lips

brings joy to our hearts…

inflamed with love toward God

and you

we become

in speaking your blessed name —

pray we shall call your name,

dear Lady,

in our time of need,

that you will be quick to intercede

with your Son

for our salvation.

Washed in the water from His side

and in His holy blood,

pray we shall rise above the sea,

beyond all rebellion,

that obedient as you, His Handmaid,

we shall find favor with the Lord

and enter into Heaven,

our names written beside your own

in the Book of Life,

dearest Mary.

September

St. John Chrysostom (September 13)

O you of golden tongue,

how well you proved

the Word of God cannot be chained;

how well you revealed

its radiance to our ears and hearts…

unconquered by threats of death

and the sufferings

the world imposes,

you proclaimed the glory of God

and His presence with us

until the very end —

pray, O dear shepherd,

who held your flock

so close to your heart

that they became one body with you

in Christ,

that we all shall be so willing

to lay down our lives,

speaking and walking in

the Word the Lord gives us

to share with all our brothers in light.

Pray indeed God's will be done

in all His holy children.

Prayers to the Saints

Our Lady of Sorrows (September 15)

O sorrowful Mother

whose heart was pierced by a sword,

who stood at the foot of the Cross

dying in spirit

as your Son died in the flesh...

Jesus was sent to suffer

and die for our sins,

and how intimately you shared

in the profound pain

He carried about all His life;

how preeminently you filled up

what was lacking in His suffering,

suffering the whole Church must share

with our crucified Lord —

pray we shall indeed enter into

the sacrifice of Christ your Son,

following in your wake,

O Mother of God;

pray we shall meet Him

along His Way of Sorrow

that His blood upon our souls

will carry us to Heaven,

where you stand at His side.

Sts. Cornelius and Cyprian
(September 16)

O brothers in Christ,

in death and in life

you gave yourselves as one

for the sake of the flock;

for the cause of the faith

readily you shed your blood

to serve the growth of God's Church —

pray we today will be zealous as you

in defending the faith with our lives;

by fasting and by prayer,

by standing courageously

before the courts of the world

and offering our flesh in sacrifice,

may we imitate you

who imitated Christ

and so come with all our brothers

to His resurrection and life.

Shepherd us well even this day

from where you now stand at the Lord's side,

that we might be unafraid to speak

and to live the truth in undying love.

O let us lay down our lives with you!

St. Robert Bellarmine (September 17)

O wise doctor

whose intellect served well

in defense of the Church

and her teachings,

who bore well the light yoke of Christ

that leads to eternal life

and shepherded your flock

in following you

along this path of our Lord —

speak to us this day

your words of grace

that the souls of all

within the Church's gates

might be founded well

on the truths of the faith

and on the love of God.

Pray we shall be wise as you

in knowing the way

the Lord marks out for His sons;

pray we shall have shepherds

so blessed with His light

that all shall be saved from the wolves about

and remain secure in the Father's arms.

St. Januarius (September 19)

O protector of your sheep,

you laid down your life

for them,

giving your blood

for the service of souls

that all might witness

the surpassing love of the Lord

and the glory that awaits

those who die in Him —

pray for shepherds

who feed their sheep,

not lording it over them

or seeking what gain they might find

for themselves,

taking the milk and wool

of their flock

and leaving them naked and lifeless…

but living the call of Christ

as you, dear shepherd, have done.

Pray those who govern God's Church

will be ready even to die for Him

and the people they serve.

Let all be protected by the blood of the Lamb.

Prayers to the Saints

Sts. Andrew Kim Taegon, Paul Chong Hasang and Companions
(September 20)

O blessed, holy martyrs

who won for yourselves

the crown of salvation

by your undying faith in God,

who cherished well

the prize of persecution

the Lord offered your souls,

who stood fast despite the death

that raged around you –

pray we shall know as you

that all the hairs of our head

are numbered by God

and in His all-embracing providence

He has care over us all,

that we might stand as strong

in our little trials

and sufferings

as you did before the face

of the executioner.

To all people be a witness to the faith

that reaches ever unto Heaven.

September

St. Matthew (September 21)

O faithful apostle

who so readily answered

the call of the Lord,

leaving your station in this world

to follow in His footsteps

and so find your place in Heaven,

who even with these first steps

brought others to the Christ

as you opened your heart

as well as your home

to Him and to the least of His brothers –

pray, dear brother through whom the Spirit has spoken,

that we too shall follow Jesus

and so find His grace and mercy,

and so find our way to the Father.

Pray our hearts will ever be

so open to hear His voice

and invite Him in to our table,

where He may eat and speak with us,

feeding us with His presence.

And pray we may be blessed as you

in drawing others to the Word, our God,

till all are one in His Body.

Prayers to the Saints

St. Pio of Pietrelcina (September 23)

O holy priest

who bore the wounds of Christ

in your hands

and in your ministry,

who served the Lord so greatly

in casting out many demons

in your confessional,

and whom He thus blessed

with miracles of the Spirit —

pray for us of lukewarm faith

who falter day to day

in following our dear Jesus' path.

So close to Him you were

in His suffering and His love;

so far are we

from His Cross and so His grace.

Pray we shall be strengthened to approach Him

and find healing for our weakness,

the frailty of our souls

which keeps us from knowing the Christ

and laying down our lives for Him

as He calls, as you have done…

O pray His blood be upon us!

Sts. Cosmas and Damian
(September 26)

O highly honored martyrs

whose tomb drew many pilgrims

and brought about many miracles,

you laid down your lives as one in the Lord,

taking up His bitter and saving cup

of suffering

all for your faith in Him and His Church,

and so, precious in His sight

was your death in His Name –

from beyond the grave

pray for us this day,

that the healing blood of Christ our Savior

be poured upon our souls,

that we too might be raised by His sacrifice,

redeemed by the death He endured;

for He has overcome the world,

and you with Him in His blood.

Pray that we who are so weak of faith

may by the Lord's grace

and your intercession

bear witness to Jesus by our own death

upon the Cross with Him.

Prayers to the Saints

St. Vincent de Paul (September 27)

O blessed help of the poor,

slave to widows and orphans

and all those most outcast

and in need,

the least of Christ's brothers

you indeed gave your life to serve,

completely spending yourself

in their assistance

and leading your own brother priests

to do the same…

and so Christ Himself you waited upon

day in and day out

upon this earth —

pray that we, too, shall be like Jesus,

filled with compassion

for the needs of our neighbors,

sharing their poverty

as we empty ourselves as the Lord has done.

May all our prayers and desires

lead to such charity for the plight of others,

that we might fulfill with you

our Savior's call to the Cross

and come, therefore, to the riches of Heaven.

St. Wenceslaus (September 28)

O faithful ruler

whose devotion served

to bring your death,

though you loved all your subjects,

caring especially for the poor,

and loved God and His Church above all,

your care and your faith

caused you to be killed

by those so jealous and selfish —

pray for us, good king,

and for the rulers in our midst,

that they will be inspired as you

with a self-effacing humility

and a desire for the truth of God's way,

giving their lives in service

of the Lord and His people,

not seeking their own gain.

Pray the Mother of God

guide all leaders

and they turn to her in obedience,

that the will of the Father shall be done

and to this world His kingdom come

by the blood of His only Son.

Prayers to the Saints

St. Lawrence Ruiz and Companions
(September 28)

O simple and devout layman,

husband and father and clerk,

suddenly you were forced to flee

your homeland and family

with your missionary companions,

but death for the faith

each one of you met

without wavering

upon disembarking in a foreign land –

pray, O blessed martyrs,

our faith shall be strong

as your own,

that should we be called

to witness even with our lives

to the faith which gives us life,

we will be ready

to enter eternity

with Christ our Lord and Savior.

If tortures threaten our bodies, too,

intercede for us for grace,

that the face of Jesus alone

we shall look upon that day.

Sts. Michael, Gabriel and Raphael
(September 29)

O mighty messengers of the Lord,

ministers of His will,

bringing His word and His power

to all poor souls on earth,

you serve to lead us unto Heaven…

you who do the bidding of God,

you who are first among those

who stand round His throne

and sing His praise,

you who are so faithful

in defending His Kingship

and keeping us from harm —

cast the devil from our midst,

instill the word of Jesus' coming

in our hearts,

bring His healing to the lost sheep,

and see that we join you

on His holy mountain on high;

carry us in your arms

to the place the Savior prepares for us

with you and all your army

in His presence.

Prayers to the Saints

St. Jerome (September 30)

O great interpreter of holy Scripture,

seeking the wisdom and power of God

you listened

to what the Lord says

in His Word

and so served to dispel

ignorance of Christ;

from your hermitage you came

to serve the Church just so,

to enlighten the minds of the faithful –

pray the Lord shall send forth today

the light of His wisdom and grace

upon those who turn to the pages

of the Word of God in prayer,

that He may be understood in truth,

that Jesus may walk amongst us again…

that knowing the Christ

we may become more like Him

and live according to His instruction,

as a lamp burning brightly in this world

to draw all men to the Lord

and the salvation of their souls,

which He so deeply desires.

OCTOBER

Prayers to the Saints
St. Thérèse of the Child Jesus (October 1)

O little flower of Jesus,

with great innocence and humility

you loved the Lord

and prayed for His Church

and especially His priests;

in all the little things of your day

you gave yourself to God's service,

and so your work reached

to the ends of the earth —

shower roses upon us from above,

where you now sit with Jesus;

teach us to walk your little way

that we might join you

with our Savior.

Pray we too might find His love

and live in His heart

as deeply as you;

pray all souls shall indeed be saved

by the blood He shed for our sake.

And pray that families

will be blessed as your own

with children who heed so well

the call of the Lord.

Guardian Angels (October 2)

O messengers of God

sent to protect and guide

us poor humans

on our way to the heavenly kingdom,

you whom He in His grace and wisdom

has appointed to carry us home,

lest we dash our foot against a stone —

keep us ever in the way of the Lord;

stay close to us,

remaining always at our side,

for we are but weak and sinful men

so prone to be led astray.

We entrust ourselves into your hands:

bring us to look upon the Father's face.

For you behold Him always,

you stand loyally in His light,

and we, how shall we gaze upon Him

without your hand to guide?

Cover us with your wings,

protect us from the heat of day

and temptation's sway

till we stand with you

in the Lord's eternal reign.

Prayers to the Saints

St. Francis of Assisi (October 4)

O image of Christ,

simple, humble, and pure,

indeed you bore the marks of Jesus

in your own body

and in your own soul;

wed to lady poverty,

you embraced loving chastity

and boasted of nothing

but the Lord alone —

pray, dear brother,

for all children of God,

for all your wayward brothers

distracted by the wealth of this world,

that we may be so blessed by the Spirit

to serve the Lord and our neighbor

as completely as you have done.

May our lives, too, be prayers

rising as a fragrant offering

unto the Lord our God

as we reflect His image in this world.

Pray our hearts be set upon Jesus

that we might follow

in His blood-soaked footsteps in joy.

St. Maria Faustina (October 5)

O apostle of mercy,

the mercy of Christ

poured freely upon all souls

for the salvation of the whole world,

especially the worst of sinners...

you suffered with our divine Lord

that souls might indeed be saved;

with His Passion you were intimate,

blessed with fellowship with Jesus

and His Mother

and vision of their presence –

pray a measure of your penitential devotion,

a drop of our Savior's holy blood,

might fall upon our hearts

and make us fruitful as you in His cause;

pray we shall be blessed

with deeper awareness of our wretchedness,

our misery,

that we might know

the infinite majesty of the Lord

and immerse ourselves and all souls

in His measureless mercy.

Let all sins be atoned for in Him!

Prayers to the Saints

St. Bruno (October 6)

O crown of contemplation

whom none excels

in solitude,

in knowing the presence of the Lord

alone in a cell,

apart from the world —

a simple chapel pray we find

in the chambers of our heart

that we might chant His praises

all the time

in the quiet,

in His sight.

Let us ever work

to discover

His breathing in our souls,

that one with Him

and with our brothers

ever we might remain.

Obedience is all we need

and He will lead us there;

then no questions will persist

as we dwell in perfect peace.

Pray such grace upon all souls.

Our Lady of the Rosary (October 7)

O Mother of prayer

and of this prayer

in which we meditate on the life

of our Lord and Savior

through your blessed intercession,

it is through you

we gain victory in Christ;

His life, death, and resurrection

become fruitful in you,

and united with you,

and so with Jesus,

we repel our enemies.

O dear Lady,

our saving Lord comes not to us

except through you:

He is born in you,

He dies with you at His side,

and He raises you to life

but to draw us all unto Himself,

that we might walk in light with Him

even in this world —

pray, yes, pray for us!

you through whom all Christians come.

Prayers to the Saints

St. Denis and Companions
(October 9)

O shepherd of a faithful people,

you shed your blood

with your brothers

as a holy offering unto the Lord

after drawing many souls

into His fold;

beheaded for your success

as Christ's evangelist,

still you lead faithful souls

to God —

pray we shall be

so ready

to lay down our own lives

for the propagation

of the Word of God,

and that on our journey

we shall be protected

from all the snares of the devil,

that nothing shall prevent

our standing at Jesus' side

both in this world

and the next.

St. John Leonardi (October 9)

O caretaker of souls

who sought so diligently

and with wisdom and love

to reform the Church

and all her members,

beginning with those in higher office,

and so were persecuted

by men who would not be healed

of their disease —

pray that all will be taught

the true doctrine of the faith,

from early childhood

to adult vocation;

may all know to what they are called

as Christians in this world.

And may that Word go forth

to the ends of the earth,

that the faith will be propagated

in all lands and in all hearts

and the Lord's holy discipline

serve as treasured guide

for all who would come

to the kingdom of Heaven.

Prayers to the Saints

St. John XXIII (October 11)

O humble and joyful Shepherd

of loving Mother Church

who desired so

to bring her balm of mercy

to a confused and bitter world,

that it might become more fully human

by imbibing of the fountain

of her life-giving doctrine

and so discover the love and peace

it so desperately seeks

in vain ideologies

that pass like mist

in the light of the Lord Jesus Christ –

pray we all find our dignity

in Christ and in the Church

He founded for our salvation;

pray the eternal Truth

She teaches in His Name

will not be obscured by Satan's wiles

but take root in the soil of Christian love

and be welcomed by all souls

who desire to possess a smile of joy

in the presence of God.

October

St. Callistus I (October 14)

O slave become Shepherd

of the universal Church,

firmly you defended her teaching

and recognized that all sins

may be forgiven

by the Lord through her;

then after serving faithfully

at the helm of Peter's bark,

you died and were buried

with your martyr brothers,

whose grave you so treasured –

pray we, too, remain firm

through all the difficult trials

and temptations of this world,

that our death may be as blessed

as your own

and we come to rest safely

in God's arms.

O that by such incorrupt faith

and unshaken courage

we too shall be raised from the dust,

from our humble origins,

to sit with our Lord in His kingdom.

Prayers to the Saints

St. Teresa of Jesus (October 15)

O teacher and Mother

who served to reform your sisters

and the lives of all Christians,

you led all souls

along the way of perfection,

which is Christ Himself —

pray his love may fill our hearts

that union with the Father

we indeed may find;

inspire us by your teaching

to seek Him

who makes His home in us...

and pray we shall have your courage,

your faith in the face of trials,

as we work to bring Him to others

and so suffer under His Cross.

Pray we shall know as you

the joy of such persecution,

which brings us only closer to God,

our spirits wed to His surpassing peace.

O pray, dear Mother,

we shall be entirely forgetful of ourselves

as we remember His presence in our lives.

St. Hedwig (October 16)

O mother of the unfortunate

and model of prayer and penance,

completely you gave yourself

to service of the Lord

and neighbor,

chastising your flesh

by constant fast and abstinence

and generously offering

your goods and your time

to all those in need —

pray we shall at least desire

to imitate your thorough devotion,

that our lives will be spent

not on things of this world

but for the reign of Heaven.

All we can do for others

let us do,

and let all be done for God,

that He alone

will rule our hearts and lives

and we will worship

Him alone,

dying to ourselves all the while.

Prayers to the Saints
St. Margaret Mary Alacoque (October 16)

O apostle of Christ's Sacred Heart,

in mystic wonder you beheld Him

and let Him wash you clean

in the streams that flow

from His Heart divine —

pray indeed we shall unite ourselves

to Jesus and His love,

that we shall submerge

our needs and sorrows

in the abyss of His mercy

and seek perfection

in union with His Sacred Heart.

There let us find salvation,

reparation for all our sins;

there let us find heavenly joy,

the peace that surpasses understanding.

With you let us enter His presence,

let us be bathed in His light,

ever progressing toward His kingdom

till we are devoted entirely

to advancing His eternal glory.

Pray His will and His way be known in us

as we entrust ourselves to His love.

October

St. Ignatius of Antioch (October 17)

O wheat of Christ

ground by the teeth of wild beasts

and so made His bread,

His leaven unto Heaven…

by such heroic witness

you became one with the Lord,

joining Him in death

and so in eternal life —

pray we shall find the strength and faith

to follow in your sacrificial footsteps,

that it will also be our sole desire

to die in Jesus' Name,

to be remade in His glory.

Teach us the way,

for it seems so dimmed

by the material things

the devil presents to our vision;

pray for us, blessed victim,

that our thirst for life in Him

will overcome any obstacle

and so our journey to His kingdom

be made straight by His grace.

His flesh and blood be our own this day.

Prayers to the Saints

St. Luke (October 18)

O bringer of the Good News,

the light of the Gospel,

to many nations…

a thorough account you have given us

of all Jesus did and taught

and of the Holy Spirit's work

among His disciples;

and so the Lord's peace

may enter our homes,

and we embrace Him with Mary —

pray, dear physician,

that the Word of the Lord

may indeed come to our hearts

through the words you declare,

and we be healed by His grace

and illumined by His Spirit;

the glory of the kingdom pray we know.

Though He has been taken from our sight,

let us proclaim His presence

with great joy,

for He yet speaks to all our souls

in the words you have recorded,

in the fire of God that guided your hand.

Sts. Isaac Jogues, John de Brébeuf and Companions (October 19)

O heroic witnesses

to the faith,

O loyal followers of Jesus

who took up the cup

of torture and death

willingly,

with desire only to join your Lord,

with delight and joy

at the deadly blows...

your offering of body and blood

is unsurpassed

because it was one

with Christ's own,

done with love for those

who killed you –

pray we shall so completely

embrace our call,

embrace the cross

provided us by the Lord,

that with your same thirst for truth

we shall lay down our lives

for our brothers.

Prayers to the Saints

St. Paul of the Cross (October 20)

O true lover of the Crucified,

always you celebrated

the feast of the Cross

in the temple of your soul,

uniting yourself with the will of God

by taking upon yourself

the torments of the Lord

in a silent joy

and so finding the food

of sacrificial love

which sustains us in this world –

pray we shall be as Christ,

that we shall walk the path

He marks out for us,

and so in embracing the Cross

find true joy in the grief we suffer,

in the blessing of oneness

with our crucified Lord

and so with His Father in Heaven.

You who have been transformed

into your Beloved,

pray we shall join you

through the Passion of Christ.

St. John Paul II (October 22)

O great Pontiff

who stood as a bulwark

against the culture of death

threatening to overtake mankind,

who served to bring down the Enemy

with the sacrifice of your life and your many works:

under the Mantle of Our Mother,

you gathered the youth of the world as one

to hear your ringing exhortation;

you enlightened minds

assailed by doubt and despair;

you taught men and women the language of love

the Lord wrought into our very bodies…

for you knew the power of the Cross

and carried it till the end,

finding light in the dark night of suffering.

The gates of Hell could not stand

against your invocation of the Spirit –

pray we too shall open wide

the doors for Christ

and fear no evil as we entrust ourselves

entirely to our Redeemer

and His Divine Mercy.

Prayers to the Saints

<u>St. John of Capistrano</u> (October 23)

O tireless preacher of God's Word,

how well, how completely,

you called all men,

and especially the priests of the Lord,

to a life of holiness,

to shine the light of Christ;

with patience and sound doctrine

and the example of a blameless life

you sought to save souls

throughout the world

and bring them into the fold

of Holy Mother Church —

pray this day apostles go forth

in the brightness of holiness

as light to the world,

drawing all men to God.

In such wisdom let truth be known,

the truth of our Savior Jesus Christ,

that every heart might call Him Lord

and proclaim the Church as His own.

Pray not a day pass,

not an hour upon this plane,

wherein His Word is not heard.

St. Anthony Mary Claret (October 24)

O zealous apostle

who traveled throughout the earth

driven by the fire of the Holy Spirit,

you labored strenuously,

rejoicing in poverty

and welcoming hardships

as you gave your very life

for the flock in your care —

pray the love of Christ

will urge us on to holy zeal

that we might approach your apostolic spirit,

desiring to inflame all men

with the fire of God's love.

Concerned always and only

for the glory of God

and the salvation of souls,

may we fulfill our call;

as sons of the Immaculate Heart of Mary,

with her same purity and commitment,

pray we give birth to Christ in souls

by the preaching of the Gospel

until all are formed in His image

in the heavenly kingdom.

Prayers to the Saints

Sts. Simon and Jude
(October 28)

O zealous and loving apostles,

to the ends of the earth

you brought the Word of the Lord;

calling sinners to repentance,

seeking healing for all souls,

you carried the light of Christ

to all the world —

pray we shall match your zeal

for the Gospel;

pray we serve to impart

the mercy of God

unto life everlasting

for all children of the Lord.

May the power and glory

upon you

in the Name of Jesus Christ

build up His Temple

in forgiveness and love

this day

that soon all will be one

with Him and with you

in Heaven.

NOVEMBER

Prayers to the Saints

All Saints (November 1)

O God's holy ones,

His apostles and martyrs,

His virgins and confessors,

all who have borne witness to Him

with your lives,

who have washed your robes

in His blood,

whose hands are clean

in His sight

and so are clothed in white,

all you who have suffered

under the Cross

in the flesh in this world

and so now stand in His light

in the Spirit

before His throne in Heaven…

O all holy ones of the Lord

from every age,

from every time and place;

from every nation you come,

speaking in every tongue

of His undying love —

please, pray for us, His pilgrim children!

November

St. Martin de Porres (November 3)

O humble and charitable soul

whose healing hands served the poor

and all those the Lord placed

in your care,

with great love you looked upon

Christ on the Cross

and in the Blessed Sacrament,

and so sought to love your neighbor

even as Jesus Himself –

pray we shall somehow learn

to put others before ourselves,

that in this way,

in the way of the Lord,

we will truly love and serve God,

knowing our sins outweigh

those of any other soul,

and yet that the mercy of our Savior

outweighs any human fault.

And so, pray we shall be as humble as you,

as kind and as caring,

that we too will lay down our lives

in prayer and in penance,

in the blood and tears of Jesus.

Prayers to the Saints

St. Charles Borromeo (November 4)

O defender of the Catholic faith

in which all the saints

make their home,

O great pastor of souls,

shepherd of Christ's flock,

who would see all enter fully

into the fold

only the saints know —

pray for the Lord's Church this day,

that it shall never turn away

from the Truth

which is at its heart,

from the Son of God

who made it,

forming it in His own blood;

pray our souls be set

on prayer to Him,

our minds on meditation

on His life,

that nothing may distract us

from His holy presence

within the walls of Mother Church

and within our own hearts.

St. Leo the Great (November 10)

O true Pastor of God's Church,

defender of the faith

from forces without

and within her walls,

you proved that this House

founded by Christ the Lord

shall never succumb

to the powers of hell

but ever stand strong

against all tides of the world

and the evil influence of the devil —

pray though the flesh be weak,

though every member be prone to sin,

that all souls set on the Rock

that is the bark of Peter

shall repel every attack

against the integrity of the faith

and stand with Jesus

as king over the flesh,

as priest offering pure sacrifice,

as prophet speaking His words…

and so until the end of time

may God's Church be ever blessed.

Prayers to the Saints

St. Martin of Tours (November 11)

O sacrificial shepherd,

you gave your life for your flock;

a poor and humble man,

you gathered the poor and humble

of the Lord

into the arms of His Church,

where they might be fed with His grace.

Ever with arms upraised

you taught your people ever to pray

and founded many houses of prayer;

peace you brought to your church

that all might serve the one true God –

pray we shall be humble and lowly

as you, dear shepherd,

and so mirror the life of our Lord.

Pray our lives be entrusted to Him,

that whatever we do be in His will;

whether we live or die,

let it not matter to us,

but only let matter the laying down of our lives,

that by such sacrificial offering

God's Word might go forth

and all souls be welcomed into Abraham's arms.

St. Josaphat (November 12)

O shepherd thirsty for souls,

whose only desire

was the unity of the Church

under Christ her King

and on the Rock of Peter...

for this cause you gave your life;

for this call from the Lord

you shed your blood —

pray this day all may be one,

that none shall shrink

from fulfilling this desire of Jesus

but by the power of the Holy Spirit

work tirelessly

and with great courage

to slake the thirst of the Lord.

We are all children of one Father;

we have but one Brother in Christ

and one Mother in the Catholic faith.

Pray this truth shall prevail

over the deceptions of the devil,

who would separate and conquer souls

but who is turned back from his evil course

when we are willing to die for one another.

Prayers to the Saints
St. Frances Xavier Cabrini (November 13)

O mother of the faith

and helper of the stranger

in the New World,

you sought with great diligence

to preserve the true religion

in a land hostile to Mother Church,

to assist those in spiritual

as well as physical need —

pray a measure of your missionary spirit

be poured out upon your daughters,

upon the many houses you established

and all those served by them.

Pray the country you took to heart

and which became your own

will turn resolutely

to the Lord and His blood

and away from the destruction

of its soul,

upon which it seems so set.

Pray the faith shall be restored

from shore to shore

and this nation in truth become

a light on a hill.

St. Albert the Great (November 15)

O patron of scientists and philosophers,

you of brilliant mind

who taught with both

human and divine wisdom,

who led your students

to deeper and purer understanding

of God and His world

and most especially His Church —

pray we partake of your teaching this day,

that the light you brought

to the minds of your flock

will not be lost

or forgotten

by eyes blind to the truth.

Pray the word upon your soul

will bring us closer to the Lord

that we might partake of Him

in sacrament and in preaching.

O how shall we see

if you do not pray for us,

if you do not serve to guide us

to the glory that surpasses

our poor ability to comprehend Him?

Prayers to the Saints

St. Margaret of Scotland (November 16)

O devout mother and queen

whose concern was ever

for your children and your people,

that they might ever be fed

in body and in soul

and so grow unto the fullness of Christ —

pray for us, O holy queen,

that we the Lord's poor subjects

might receive from His hand

all we need

to become His sons and daughters.

In prayer and gratitude

let us remain ever before His throne,

that by such holy fear

we might be made fruitful as you,

bearing children unto Him

and raising them to His glory.

A heart for the poor

may we ever nourish

that, as poor as we are,

by our King's gracious blessing

we might give what He provides

until all enter His reign.

November

St. Gertrude (November 16)

O blessed mystic of Jesus,

you were saved by Him

from a life of vain pursuit

of the things and thoughts

of this world

to find union with His Sacred Heart,

which holds all heavenly treasures.

You see Him now

(do you not, dear virgin?)

in His perfection,

even as you saw Him,

though only in the shadow of vision,

here upon this plane –

pray we shall also know

His blessed perfection,

the beating of His Sacred Heart

within our own,

the love which surpasses all understanding

illumining our soul…

that no more will we ever desire

than to be with Him

where you are now,

in His eternal glory.

Prayers to the Saints

St. Elizabeth of Hungary (November 17)

O charitable soul

who gave all you owned

for the sake of the Gospel,

though endowed with great riches

you embraced lady poverty

that you might serve the Lord

with a heart beating for the poor.

With your own hands

you tended the sickest;

into your own home

you welcomed the most destitute —

pray that in our small way

we too may follow

in the footsteps of Christ

and give our lives

to the poor whom He loves

and to prayer in His presence.

Pray our hearts, too,

may know His tender care for souls

and our own souls

meditate upon Him night and day;

pray we too shall give up all

to find His holy kingdom.

November

St. Rose Philippine Duchesne (November 18)

O woman who prayed always

and had great mercy on souls,

whose missionary zeal

led you across the ocean,

thousands of miles from your home,

to educate the poor

and care for the sick,

to bring the love of Jesus

to those most in need —

pray we too shall have a heart

set on service of the Lord

and remembrance of His presence,

that our concern for those apart from Christ

will drive us to great ends,

even to the ends of the earth,

where certainly He dwells.

Pray we shall have your courage

in facing the unknown,

in calling all home

to the Heart of God;

and through all we do for Him

let us remain in prayer,

knowing His Heaven here on earth.

Prayers to the Saints

Presentation of Mary (November 21)

O holy Temple of the Lord,

preeminent member of His Church,

you who were destined from all ages

to bear the Son of God,

to be His chosen dwelling place…

you were weaned into His Temple;

there you ever remained,

becoming yourself the House of God,

where He now ever stays —

pray we be built into His Temple;

pray we become sons and daughters

unto you.

In you let us make our home, dear Mother,

that the holiness of Jesus

we shall ever share.

We cannot live in Him

if apart from you;

we cannot be as Christ's Body,

blessed by the Holy Spirit

and doing the Father's will on earth,

if you are not our Mother,

if you are not the Temple in which we dwell.

Pray our holiness mirror your own.

St. Cecilia (November 22)

O holy virgin and martyr,

you sang a song of love to Jesus,

a song that could not be dimmed,

could not be taken away,

for you were protected

by an angel of the Lord

and willing to give your life

to maintain your love for Him —

pray for us poor souls

of this day and age

from whom purity is so far removed,

who need deep conversion to believe,

to see the angel at your side,

to know the path

to which the Lord calls us,

the Cross which is every Christian's song.

So far removed, so far removed are we,

and so impassable is the way to Him…

inspire in our souls, dear saint,

the desire for the incorruptible

that beat in your heart,

that we too might sing a song to Jesus

pleasing to His ears.

Prayers to the Saints

St. Clement I (November 23)

O successor to Peter,

Shepherd of God's Church,

Father of all the churches

in the Body of Christ,

these you instructed well;

these you gave a shepherd's care...

for these and for the Lord

you shed your blood —

pray for God's Church even this day,

that she shall remain united

under her one Lord and Savior,

each member serving the good of all

as wholly as you have done.

Pray we all work together in Jesus' Name

and in His blood

to do the Father's will

and so become as holy as He,

as holy as you were blessed to become.

Pray the teaching of the apostles

ever ring in our ears

that we shall never forget

the way the Christ marks out for us,

the way of truth that leads to life.

November

St. Columban (November 23)

O father of holy monasteries

who dug deeply in the earth,

in the heart of man,

and laid their foundation

on the Rock that is Christ

that they might be made in His image,

in the image of Him who created us –

pray we shall love the Lord as He commands

and so be holy as He is holy,

truly reflecting the image of our God

and living in His surpassing peace.

Pray austerity serve well

to make us in the Lord's image,

to purge from us all that is not of Him;

may we be blessed to serve

with untiring devotion and care

the will of our Lord in all things,

in worship of Him, in prayer,

and in genuine love of our neighbor,

that the Gospel may go forth

to the ends of the earth

not just in words

but in our very flesh and blood.

Prayers to the Saints

St. Andrew Dung-Lac and Companions
(November 24)

O you who were martyred

over three centuries of persecution

in a country so bitter toward the faith,

bishops and priests and laymen alike,

native to the land and foreign-born,

all innocent souls

who suffered even torture in joy,

all for the sake of the Lord and His Church —

pray we shall be as ready as you

to bear witness to the faith

with our lives,

that all as one in the Body of Christ

we will be willing even

to die

to satiate our thirst for the kingdom

and for the salvation of souls.

O what joy to be as Jesus,

to walk in His steps

even to the Cross!

No greater blessing could any soul know

on this corrupted plane...

Pray we shall come with you to Heaven.

November

St. Catherine of Alexandria (November 25)

O virgin pure and brilliant,

you gave your life

in defense of the faith,

refuting all arguments to its contrary;

though you were but a child yourself,

you stood strong before your tormentors,

enduring the persecution and torture

they struggled in vain to muster against you,

ever shining the light of purity and truth

before their corrupted minds and hearts –

pray for those who defend the faith

and all those who would explain it away,

that the light of pure reason

will dispel all doubt and darkness

and the verity of the faith be known

by all souls on this earth,

undeniable as it is

by the mind of any man.

Pray we not waste words or time

but live a holy life before God,

giving witness to His presence

in the world and in the Church,

and come finally to rest on His mountain.

Prayers to the Saints

St. Andrew (November 30)

O brother of the Rock of our Church,

you who brought him to our Lord,

you who were crucified

on the Cross of our Savior,

who shed your blood

freely for His cause…

you who thirsted for His coming

and welcomed Him so readily

into your life —

bring us also to the Messiah's side

and pray we shall receive Him

as well as your brother has done;

pray we, too, will abandon our boats,

our moorings in this world,

to follow the Christ

along the way He leads,

even apart from home and family.

Brothers to the Son pray we become,

accomplishing the Father's will

with our lives;

capture us in His net this day

that we too might stand in His light

with all the redeemed of Israel.

DECEMBER

Prayers to the Saints

St. Francis Xavier (December 3)

O holy apostle of the Lord,

model of faith in God

and love of the Church,

has there been a soul

to match your zeal

for the salvation of the world?

Convict us of our laziness,

of our sloth,

of our distraction by the things

not of the kingdom of God;

of what worth are our lives

if not spent in service of the Lord

and of neighbor?

O missionary of missionaries,

by your prayer

let the Church on earth,

which flounders so in empty illusion,

be renewed by a living faith

that reaches to the ends of the world

and banishes all darkness

from the hearts and minds of men.

Pray God's kingdom come

and reign amongst us.

December

St. John of Damascus (December 4)

O blessed teacher of the faith —

may the nourishing waters of our Mother,

of the true teaching of our Church,

flow upon all souls,

calling them to the Lord

from whom they emanate;

like the waters trickling from the temple

in Ezekiel's vision,

may they grow and increase

as they travel to the ends of the earth,

making all whole,

pure in the light of God.

Pray that the Mother of Heaven,

through whom flow these waters,

these graces pouring forth

from the Cross of Christ…

will pray for us here on earth

and see that we are nourished well

by the faith

brought to us by the holy apostles

and still fostered

by the shepherds of the Church.

May the Lord keep us in His way.

Prayers to the Saints

St. Nicholas (December 6)

O bishop of Myra,

shepherd of the Lord's sheep

who has with a generous heart

cared so well

for His little ones…

all became as your children,

for you loved your flock

with the love of Christ Himself;

their needs were your own —

pray our hearts will be like yours,

that just so generously

we will give to those in need,

provide for those in our care.

I pray you will see us now

as your children here

and beg the bearer of all good gifts

to provide for all those most in need,

that in joy all souls

may welcome His coming,

ready for the joys of Heaven.

May our love be one

with the love of our Good Shepherd,

now and in eternity.

St. Ambrose (December 7)

O good bishop

and wise doctor of the Church —

pray for us,

that the water that is Christ

might pour upon our souls,

especially His chosen apostles,

your fellow bishops,

and fill all with wisdom from on high,

leading us away from all lies

to the truth that is Jesus.

Pray our hearts shall be filled

to overflowing

with this Word,

that the Gospel might be preached

by lips anointed

with the Body and Blood of our Lord;

may the darkness of error

be dispelled

and God's pure light

shine in our midst.

Pray for us, good doctor,

pray for us;

lead us indeed to the truth that is Christ.

Prayers to the Saints

Immaculate Conception (December 8)

O pure Mother,

you are she who is full of grace;

it is you who have found the Lord's favor.

Preserved from all sin from the womb,

overflowing with all His blessings,

you are the hope of our race,

the one created soul most like to God —

pray for us this day, dear Mother,

that we might be kept from the snares of the world,

from the enticements of the devil.

O help us be pure as you,

obedient to the will of the Father,

bringing His Son into this world

by the Holy Spirit's power.

You who now reign in Heaven

with the Lord, your only Son,

intercede for us who toil on earth

that we too might enter God's presence;

you who are blessed to be one with Him,

pray the Church you bear be so well founded.

Hail, Full of Grace!

Your Name be blessed forever

by all generations.

December

St. Juan Diego (December 9)

O humble child of the Lord

whom Our Lady blessed

with her presence,

to whom she gave

roses in winter —

pray for us who are not humble as you,

whose obedience is cold

and grown so weak,

that she might come to us, too,

that she might speak a word to our hearts

and we might as children

listen

and do as she directs,

she who directs us only to Jesus,

only to His love.

Pray this continent be once again

renewed

by the grace of God;

may Our Lady's image

be upon our hearts

that we too might proclaim

the glory of the Lord

and His love for His children.

Prayers to the Saints

St. Damasus I (December 11)

O Bishop of Rome

who guided the bark of Peter

through difficult waters,

who kept her on the course

set for her by the Lord

even as she grew in this world

from a Church of the blood of martyrs

to one entering the light of day,

of acceptance by the city of man…

you who sought so diligently

to preserve the memory of the martyrs

lest it should pass away,

and the Cross of Christ

with it —

pray that today, too,

the Church will remember its root,

the root of Jesse and His sacrifice,

and that as she grows

our Mother on earth

will be well understood

by those called into her walls.

Pray the martyrs pray for us,

that in their blood we always find our growth.

December

Our Lady of Guadalupe (December 12)

O Patroness of the Americas

and Protectress of the Unborn,

look upon our troubled state,

where lust and greed abound,

where thousands are killed in the womb

every day,

where the poor and the rich

are separated by steel walls

and thirsting souls

die in the desert —

help us, dear Mother,

to discover life,

to find your guidance

in this land of opportunity

and broken dreams,

in these hearts that have grown so cold

that more children are sacrificed

on unholy altars

than when you first came

to turn our hearts to the Lord!

Pray for us, Our Lady,

or we shall surely die

in a soulless pride.

Prayers to the Saints

St. Lucy (December 13)

O bride of our Lord Jesus Christ,

in your virginity

and in your dying

you have given yourself

entirely

to the Lord of Heaven and earth.

O how like Him you were

in your purity

and in your suffering!

and so how close to Him

you must be

in Heaven —

pray that a ray of His light

might come to us

who sit in darkness,

we whose hearts

are not as strong

as your own.

His heavenly light

we wish to enter;

by your prayers

may we see

His glory.

December

St. John of the Cross (December 14)

O mystical doctor —

help us by way of the Cross

to find wisdom and knowledge of Christ

and union with God;

let us desire to enter

the suffering of the Lord,

that by this means

we may draw closer

to His glorious presence

and there remain in joy.

Let us fear not

the dark night the soul must endure

but bear it well,

that we might be purged of all blindness;

pray the Lord will shine upon us

His holy light

and we might soon look upon

His face

with you.

May the Lord's Cross overshadow all

and anoint every soul

with the peace that surpasses understanding,

with His undying love.

Prayers to the Saints

St. Peter Canisius (December 21)

O great defender of the faith,

of the clear waters,

the wellspring of salvation

that flows from the Sacred Heart

of our Savior

into His holy Church,

thus to nourish the world

and fill it with truth

and wisdom

and love…

you whom the Lord inspired

with apostolic zeal

to teach and lead souls

along His holy way —

teach us today

by your gracious intercession

to be faithful,

to be obedient to the voice of Jesus

and the Spirit speaking in the Mother

the Lord God provides His pilgrim people.

Let us not be separated from His Word

and His precious Body and Blood,

but come together as one in His presence.

St. John of Kanty (December 23)

O holy teacher of the faith

and pastor of Christ's flock

who instructed with wisdom

and led by kindness and humility

those in your care

and all those around you —

teach us today

not only to know our faith

but to practice it by holiness of life

as you have done,

so simply,

so thoroughly as a child of the Lord.

Pray for us

and pray for our priests,

for whom you are a model of perfection.

All yourself you have given

in imitation of Jesus;

may the Lord God

be in our hearts and on our lips

just so truly

as He has been

with you,

good teacher.

St. Stephen (December 26)

O first martyr,

model of Christ's love

and bearer of His Holy Spirit

in wisdom and in truth,

you who spoke as the Lord Himself

and died as He died,

with the forgiveness of your persecutors

upon your lips

and utter trust of the Father

in your heart —

pray that we too

will find the grace and strength

to commend our lives

into the Father's hands,

never holding bitterness

toward those who destroy the body,

who would chain the Word,

but ever loving every soul

even as you have done.

O let our hearts be set on Jesus!

Let them bleed as His own,

that united in Heaven with Him we shall be

with you in the glory of God.

St. John (December 27)

O beloved disciple of the Lord

who saw Him

and touched Him,

who believed in Him

with all your being,

who loved Him so

that no love but His

surpassed your own —

speak to us this day

of the Word of life

who has come among us,

died for us,

and been raised from the grave.

Continue to proclaim that love

which alone saves men from sin,

which alone banishes death from our midst;

let us share in your love for Jesus

and in the joy you knew so well

join you in proclaiming

Him who has come.

Point us to Jesus even this day,

that we too might see

and believe.

Prayers to the Saints

Holy Innocents (December 28)

O innocent martyrs of the Christ

who gave your lives

from the cradle

for Him who carries the Cross,

who suffered and died in His place

even before His crucifixion,

even as His martyrs would do

after His death on the Tree —

let our hearts cry not

for the evil that has wrought

your violent death;

pray we not fear

the dark wrath of this world's king

but set our hearts

on the joy of our Lord's kingdom,

where you now reign with Him

and to which we hope to come

by the laying down of our own lives

in His Name.

And pray for the least among us

who suffer the most this day,

that they who are murdered in the womb

will know the light of Christ's holy face.

December

St. Thomas Becket (December 29)

O blessed martyr

who died in the cathedral,

murdered by the king of this world

as you defended the Chair of Peter

and the true faith of the Church –

where can we find bishops like yourself;

how shall the Church be led

without holy apostles

willing to give their lives

as Christ,

in whose place they stand?

Pray for us, devout shepherd,

that many will be inspired

by your example

to follow in the footsteps of our Lord

and defend the faith

even unto the shedding of blood,

for what is the shedding of blood in this world

compared with the light of Heaven

you now know in our Savior's presence?

Pray for us and let us pray with you,

seeking truth and love

in our pilgrimage on this earth.

Prayers to the Saints

Holy Family

(Sunday in the Octave of Christmas or December 30)

O three holy persons

united as one

in the humble home

at Nazareth,

Mary and Joseph

with God's only Son…

who became your Son,

who became our Son,

who became our Brother

in all things human

and shared with you

the food of your table

and the dust beneath your feet —

you are our model upon this earth;

you we should follow

to find new birth in the Spirit,

to find ourselves sons of the Father,

to be as brother to Christ.

O Holy Family,

what a blessed trinity you form

in the love of God and neighbor;

pray we not fall short of your grace.

St. Sylvester I (December 31)

O eminent Shepherd

of God's people

who led us from the catacombs

into the light of day

by a blessed peace

with the city of man,

allowing the Lord's Church

to grow and flourish freely

in its sacraments,

in its worship of the one true God —

pray the Body of Christ

may again prosper in truth

with its divine Head,

that the Light that has come into the world

may be proclaimed to the ends of the earth

and all souls called by the Lord

come to the font of Baptism

and find the fullness of faith

in the holy Catholic Church.

Pray there be no dissension

in the Body

but that all shall be one in Him

who is God Himself.

OTHER BOOKS by JAMES KURT

"TURN and Become like Children":
Refuting the Presumed Contradictions of
the Jerusalem Bible Old Testament Commentary —
A case study in the problems afflicting modern Biblical scholarship.   188 pp.   2019.

"Into Your Hands...":
Distillation of the Letters of Fr. Jean-Pierre de Caussade —
Reflections of the profound counsel of Fr. De Caussade to embrace the Cross
and find the Lord's will (and joy) even in our greatest sufferings.   82 pp.   2019

Remembrance of Things Present —
A mystical work seeking the presence of the LORD in the moment,
where He dwells at all times.   100 pp.   2018.   w/ imprimatur.

Two Books: Paradox and the Christian Faith / Hippie Convert —
The apparent contradictions of the Faith are explained for those who seek wisdom;
and a member of the flower generation addresses true love and peace,
in poetic form.   238 pp.   2016.   w/imprimatur.

Lines of Grace: Meditations on Verses of Holy Scripture,
The Stations of the Cross, and The Most Holy Rosary —
A Catholic devotional especially for the encouragement of the practice of plenary
indulgence.   195 pp.   2016.

Christian Vision of the Old Testament —
Synopsis and exhortation; faith-filled overview of all books of the Old Testament
as prefiguration of Jesus, with a focus on the prophetic nature of God's Word.
273 pp.   2013.   w/ imprimatur.

Blessed Guilt: A Universal Conversion Story —
On the life-giving repentance found in Jesus' blood;
vaguely autobiographical but without particulars.   119 pp.   2013.   w/ imprimatur.

Chapters of the Gospels —
Exposition of the four gospels, chapter by chapter;
in the style of *Our Daily Bread*.   114 pp.   2009.   w/ imprimatur.

The Most Holy Trinity and the Four Corners of the Universe —
A collection of writings on the Trinity and its reflection in Creation;
founded upon the Shema. 300 pp. 2008. w/ imprimatur.

YHWH: Order of the Divine NAME —
On the significance of the contemplative silence that is the NAME of God,
and its application to a spiritual life. 260 pp. 2008. w/ imprimatur.

Our Daily Bread: Exposition of the Readings of Catholic Mass —
A page of writing for every Mass of the liturgical calendar for the Roman Rite;
reflections drawn from the readings themselves. 727 pp. 2004. w/ imprimatur.
Our Daily Bread: Lent — 86 pp.   2019. w/ imprimatur.

Turn of the Jubilee Year: A Conversion Song —
Autobiographical depiction of vocation search through pilgrimage to Medjugorje
and stays at a hermitage or two. 230 pp. 2004.

Songs for Children of Light: Ten Albums of Lyrics —
A white on black conceptual work with simple drawings for each song.
150 pp. 2003.

silence in the city —
Short contemplative poems; moments of divine silence in the midst of city life.
148 pp. (74 pieces). 2003.

www.ingramcontent.com/pod-product-compliance
Lightning Source LLC
Chambersburg PA
CBHW052019070526
44584CB00016B/1825